to knot | or not

To Libby –

I hope you enjoy the insight into marriage that these wonderful women share.

Blessings to you –

Anna Greene

November 7, 2007

"Proverbs 11:14 (KJV) says, 'Where no counsel is, the people fall: but in the multitude of counsellors there is safety.'" *To Knot or Not* wonderfully displays this verse with an abundance of advice. It unravels myriads of questions a woman may have about marriage and ties them together with the personal stories from women who delightfully share their marriage experiences."

—Sandy Lovern, author of *Engaged! A Devotional to Help a Bride-to-Be Navigate Down the Aisle*

to knot | or not

HONEST ADVICE
from MARRIED WOMEN

Donna Margaret Greene

NEW HOPE
PUBLISHERS

Birmingham, Alabama

New Hope® Publishers
P. O. Box 12065
Birmingham, AL 35202-2065
www.newhopepublishers.com

New Hope Publishers is a division of WMU®.

Library of Congress Cataloging-in-Publication Data

Greene, Donna Margaret, 1947-
  To knot or not : honest advice from married women / Donna Margaret Greene.
    p. cm.
  ISBN 978-1-59669-093-6 (sc)
  1. Wives--Religious life. I. Title.
  BV4528.15.G74 2007
  248.8'435--dc22

                                2007024856

ISBN-10: 1-59669-093-3
ISBN-13: 978-1-59669-093-6
N074141• 1107 • 5M1

dedication

To married couples who have

purposed to stay married

for better and for worse,

in sickness and in health.

May they share the gift of oneness

until parted by death.

contents

acknowledgments

Thank you to all the women who contributed to this book. I thank you for your insights, for being vulnerable and honest, and for the time and effort you put forth to make *To Knot or Not* possible.

Many of the contributors grew up in Community Ministry for Girls. I am blessed to have been a part of your weddings and have the privilege of observing your marriages and, in many cases, getting to know your children. Thank you for hanging in when the going gets tough—for working hard to make your marriages a little piece of "heaven on earth." May you be richly rewarded.

Thank you to all who shared anonymously. I know that your courage will encourage many.

A very special thank-you to New Hope Publishers. I am so blessed to be one of your authors. I appreciate your love for women and desire that they have tools, in the form of books, to help them grow and become all that God intends for them to be.

Thank you to Andrea Mullins, the publisher, who continues to let me write "outside the box" and move with God's leading concerning topics.

Thank you to Cathy Butler and Joyce Dinkins, my editors, who read and polished each word and made the book come to life. Thank you also to Sherry Hunt, interior page designer; and Kathryne Solomon, copy editor.

Thank you to Tina Atchenson for her skills in marketing and help in making the book known.

Thank you to Tamzen Benfield for her help in keying in the manuscript and careful eye in editing.

Thank you to all who work at New Hope. Your efforts in varied ways make all the books possible.

Although no longer with New Hope, a special thanks goes to Rebecca England, my former editor, and Tara Miller, former marketing director. You two really got me off to a great start in writing books. You listened to all my ideas and let me run fast and hard. Thank you! I will always consider you great friends and will forever be thankful for you.

> "Now, may this little Book a blessing be
> To those who love this little Book and me,
> And may its buyer have no cause to say
> His money is but lost or thrown away."
> —John Bunyan (1628–1688)

(the author's blessing to the reader from the preface to the second part of *The Pilgrim's Progress*)

TO GOD BE THE GLORY!

introduction

As the founder and director of Community Ministry for Girls, a faith-based, service-oriented, interdenominational Bible study program which is now in its 35th year with well over 3,800 girls having participated, weddings have become a normal part of life.

For me, a regular weekend includes a wedding, an engagement party, a shower, rehearsal dinner, or bridesmaids luncheon. I have no idea how many weddings I have attended, but would say that close to 1,000 would not be an exaggeration. I do know that a record was set when I was invited to 52 in one year. I try to attend some function for each bride, often juggling weddings and receptions. My personal record was making some part of four weddings in one day. I have walked the aisle as a bridesmaid more times than I can count. I had an attic full of dresses before I realized that I really would never wear those bridesmaid dresses again. Presently I do have a closet fully devoted to wedding and party clothes. I have cut hundreds of cakes, prayed with numerous brides, and read Scripture from the pulpits of almost every denomination. Sometimes I feel like the professional wedding guest.

While writing *twentysomething girl* and spending so much time with young women in that decade of their lives, I was brought face-to-face with those now married and, for the most part, those wishing to be married. I listened and observed and the idea for *To Knot or Not* came about.

With such a large group to work with, the news spread and advice on engagements, weddings, and early years of marriage began to pour in.

It is important to know that most of the contributors are listed in the back of the book. But, in some cases advice was shared by those who wished to remain anonymous. It was important to them that their stories be shared while at the same time protecting their husbands.

Also, note should be taken that not all of the women who wrote are in their 20s, but each one has been married less than ten years.

Names are used in special cases that connect special stories with the actual person who is sharing it.

one

Marriage—
Your Way or God's Way?

"For this reason a man will leave his father and mother and be united to his wife, and they will become one flesh."
—Genesis 2:24

Marriage is a gift from God, created by God, and meant for enjoyment, fulfillment, and the procreation of children. We've heard this pronouncement many times in the wedding homily before the minister closes the ceremony with, "I now pronounce you husband and wife." God ordained marriage to be a covenant between one man and one woman until death would separate them. It's a serious commitment, and yet the divorce rate continues to climb in America. What is happening? Aside from accepting Christ as Savior, who you marry or who you choose not to marry affects your life more than any other decision.

Marriage should be for better or worse, and it should be for keeps. How important to follow the Lord's leading and to be guarded through the principles set forth in Scripture. God promises to give only His very best to those who leave the choice up to Him.

"Trust in the Lord with all your heart and lean not on your own understanding; in all your ways acknowledge him, and he will make your paths straight."

—Proverbs 3:5–6

So, how do you know when you've found *the one?*

A 23-year-old woman who has been married one year shares her reflections on this question.

Growing up, I dreamed about the type of man I would marry. I dreamed that we would have a passionate and romantic relationship that was seasoned daily with breath-stopping moments and a constant sense of awe and wonder. Admittedly, most all of us progress out of this stage . . . to some degree. But the form I have seen this same expectation and mind-set take in young women's lives is something like this: Dating a guy for some time, she begins to wonder, *Is he* the one? This question pervades her thoughts and is sometimes concluded with a wistful, romantic, and completely unrealistic answer of *I just knew.* For many couples, perhaps there has been a moment of just knowing, but from my own experience, as well as from the deep and honest thoughts of all the wives and fiancées I have talked to, discovering *the one* for you is not quite so dramatic.

Most of us are mature enough to realize that the man of our dreams takes somewhat of a different form when we look at real-life men. Search for the rest of your life to find a man who meets every one of your wishes, and I'd love to see who you come up with. I think the Lord would never provide that person (if he exists!) because His plan for us is always different—and better (whether or not we realize it)—than what we would choose for ourselves. But how are we to know?

This 23-year-old goes on to share guidelines that gave her discernment in choosing the man God would have to be her husband.

- Make sure I am on God's intended path for my life. Am I choosing the path that best enables me to be more like the woman Christ calls me to be?
- If the path is right, then my heart is in a position to hear God's guidance.
- If in a relationship with a man whose desire is to be all God intends for him to be, the answer to, "Could he be someone I could marry?" is yes.
- The deciding factor to the question, "Is he *the one* for me?" becomes the decision itself.

Marriage is an unconditional commitment to an imperfect person. Because it is a commitment, why should the decision to be married be any different? Her conclusion:

We commit our lives every day to loving our spouse *actively* and *decisively*, and it seems only fitting that our contemplation of whether or not to marry that person boils down to a commitment as well. You will always be able to find reasons not to be with someone, and you will always find areas in your relationship that are not perfect. Thank goodness! To have a true, realistic, and daily-thriving relationship with another imperfect person means to be committed to making it work. Though the Lord's hand is most surely in every aspect of not only allowing the relationship to commence, but for allowing it to continue as well, it is our active decisiveness that determines whom we will marry. If in place is a heart that constantly seeks after the Lord's intention for who we are called to be, then He delights in a firm and decisive commitment that says, "You *are the one* for me, not because I just knew but because I am deciding to commit my life to you."

Another young woman who has been married ten years shares the story of God drawing her husband to her without warning.

> With regard to Mr. Right . . . I am a believer that God has someone picked out for each of us and that all we need to do is remain patient and focused on Him and He will reveal to us a love beyond our best dreams.

Her story reveals the fact that through college and afterward, she dated the wrong guy.

I knew for years that he was *not* the right guy for me, but for silly reasons I kept dating him. It became convenient and comfortable. I wanted so badly to help him. I wanted him to know God and love Him like I did. I wanted to change him into being the right guy for me, but I knew he wasn't and never would be. My journals were filled with prayers about this young man—asking God to change him or bring to me the man that He wanted me to marry.

A couple of years later I began working in another city and met a guy from New York City. I thought of him so highly. I loved being around him as we worked together, becoming good friends. I prayed for him. In the beginning it was for little things. I prayed for his days, for projects he was working on, for his success. I found myself praying for his heart. Did he know God? I prayed for his happiness and joy. Then it hit me! I was falling in love with the guy! Without warning, really, God showed me the most wonderful man I had ever met.

This young man later asked her to dinner, as he was moving to Pennsylvania with his job. He had written her a letter that he would give her when he moved.

She couldn't stand the suspense. *What was in the letter?* she thought. After persistent asking, he finally told her the letter spoke of his love for her. He had fallen in love with her from afar and wanted to spend forever with her.

I started to cry and admitted that I had fallen in love with him too. That is how our relationship started: no dating, not one kiss, ever! Nothing. We left the restaurant that night, got in our separate cars, and drove home to our apartments. My quiet time that night was a doozy! *God, what in the world just happened? I just told him that I loved him. What was I thinking? But I do love him! How can I love someone that I don't know that well? But I do know him so well from our talks, our sharing, and our friendship.*

God had surprised this young woman with a love she did not imagine.

I was trying so hard to think about that perfect love that it didn't even occur to me God had given it to me without me realizing it.

The next weekend she took him home to meet her parents but didn't tell them she was in love with him until after the weekend was over. Sunday night, after calling to say she had returned safely to her apartment, she added, "You know that young man I brought home? Well, I am going to marry him!" Less than three months later, he proposed, and five months later they were married.

Her advice:

- Trust the Lord with your mate.
- Be friends. (We were friends first and remain friends ten years later.)
- Be each other's cheerleader, supporter, assistant, confidant, well-wisher—all in one.
- Put your spouse before yourself.
- Pray that God will make him all he is to be.

- Enjoy and concentrate on each other before having children.
- Always act like you love each other as much as you truly do.

After ten years of marriage she concludes:

> It sounds so simple, but life gets busy, babies multiply, stress comes out of nowhere, and you are running on empty. Don't forget to put your spouse first.
>
> Marriage is the best thing that has *ever* happened to me or for me! It is definitely God's intricate design and plan—completely created by Him alone!

For many, marriage is the fulfillment of lifelong dreams and prayers. It is exciting and exhilarating, but at the same time very real. Getting married is a time of growth, change, and blending of two very different human beings. It is a learning experience. Marriage is God's timing for two people to learn, mature, and grow.

A wife of three years writes:

> God knew it would be better to have the two of us together than apart. Yes, I was content single for many reasons, but God knew the longing of the depths of my heart and soul. He knew it was best for me not to be alone. My husband and I are better people together. Growing pains become the biggest, hardest, and best thing about being

married. I have learned more about myself since I got married than ever before in my life. Sharing, and being vulnerable and transparent, has shown me things that I had denied or never even knew existed. Marriage is a very tough and ever-changing experience, but oh, it is worth it.

"Delight yourself in the Lord and he will give you the desires of your heart. Commit your way to the Lord; trust in him and he will do this. . . . Be still before the Lord and wait patiently for him."

—Psalm 37:4, 5, 7

If God's best for you is marriage and the players are in place, the obvious progression leads to engagement.

Engagement

two

"So Jacob served seven years to get Rachel, but they seemed like only a few days to him because of his love for her."
—Genesis 29:20

Getting engaged! It happens quickly when he pops the question; slowly as you grow to know each other better and become more confident of each other's love; or it happens with grandeur, planned in exciting, romantic ways. It does not matter how it happens, getting engaged sets in motion a whirlwind of plans and emotions that heightens daydreams and catapults you into the future.

Parties, plans, and the wonderful feeling of being the bride are a few things to look forward to once the news begins to spread. Family and friends should be told first, but great news like a wedding doesn't take long to travel far and wide.

A newly engaged 23-year-old writes, "Already I have realized how humbling engagement time can be. So many people go out of their way to send cards, presents, and attend parties. One of my friends threw a small party for us shortly after we got engaged. At that time we both realized it was the first party held in our honor since we turned 12. Everyone's generosity has helped my fiancé and me realize the magnitude of this special time in our lives. We've also realized the importance of showing that same generosity to others who are in similar situations."

Being in love and becoming engaged do not necessarily coincide. Waiting for that proposal can be brutal.

It only took a month for me to realize that my boyfriend was *the one*. From the way he encouraged me in my life and my Christian walk, it was clear that God made him perfectly for me. It wasn't long before he revealed feeling the same way. However, the timing wasn't right because he had a job in one city and I was still in graduate school in another city. We would be living in separate towns for a year and a half. It was during this frustrating time that God taught me about patience. I knew my boyfriend was *the one* for me, but I also realized that I must wait until he felt God leading him to take that next step. This anticipation and anxiety felt while waiting for the proposal was difficult. I couldn't talk with my girlfriends about him as my future husband without people making comments about how he had yet to propose. I was eager to begin the planning process, but refused to be that girl who pressures her boyfriend into buying a ring. Finally, I decided to ask God for patience and contentment in the relationship. I learned to trust Him and His plans. After turning it over to God, a proposal came three weeks later!

Sometimes an engagement requires a lot of waiting and then a proposal can come at a most unexpected moment. Such is the case of a newly married 23-year-old.

There are two things I've always desired to be: a wife and a doctor. Silly as it seems, those have been the desires of my heart for as long as I can remember. There are countless times the Lord has patiently listened to the prayers of His child, "Father, if it is in Your will, please allow me to devote my life to my family and allow my life's work to be helping others as a physician." As I graduated from college, and continued to date the love of my life, neither engaged to be married nor accepted into medical school, I began to doubt the Lord's sovereign plan—things just weren't happening in my timing. The months following graduation seemed like years as I felt that I had no direction where my life was heading. It was then that the Lord answered my prayers. One Friday afternoon in late July I was accepted into medical school and was to start school in less than two weeks in a new city, one I had only visited briefly. Terrified and yet relieved, I called my friends and family explaining the way the Lord had answered my prayers. The very next day, on a trip to Auburn for my 22nd birthday, my boyfriend proposed on a date he had been planning since the beginning of the summer. Excited and full of awe with what the Lord had done, I once again called the same friends and family to explain to them the amazing way the Lord had fulfilled all of my dreams in such a short time. I moved to Mobile, Alabama, to start medical school two weeks later—humbled with a new appreciation for the power of our sovereign Lord.

God began to move on this young woman's behalf as her fiancé's company agreed to transfer him to a city close to the medical school she would be attending. The new bride concludes, "If I have learned anything in my years on this earth thus far, it has been to pray diligently and with expectation of what the Lord will bring. As I look forward to what my marriage and my future career will hold, I am filled with anticipation because I realize that yielding to the will of the Lord will bring blessings beyond the imagination."

Engagements can be as long or as short as the couple desires. Planning can be extensive, but sometimes marriage comes quickly.

I had been dating a wonderful man for a short time. I obviously found him to be a strong Christian, interesting, and genuine . . . anyway, after I saw just how good he was with my grandfather, I realized he was *the one*! It was like he had passed the test. We continued to date and dated only nine or ten months before we got engaged! How fun . . . to be getting married . . . to actually be living the reality of my dream! So, upon getting engaged, we flirted with different dates and locations according to what we really wanted. The most important aspect of the decision for me was that I wanted my grandfather to be present at our wedding. At the time we had gotten engaged, Papa was really sick with two different types of cancer. It was one blessing that Papa had met the man of my dreams, but it was another for him to actually be a part of our union. Therefore, my fiancé and I scheduled our wedding for three months later. Sure, that makes for a very, very short engagement, which is really nice, but since Papa's health was declining quite rapidly, I wanted to make certain that Papa could be a part because he is such an important person in my life. What a blessing to have met my fiancé, who understood the situation completely and who also felt it was important to want such a short engagement. It's sad at times that people might suspect that we have a "bun in the oven," whereas if they really knew the extent of the story, then they might have thought otherwise. It is so vital to figure out what it is that is important to you; for me, that is my family and my grandfather. It is then that you can make such decisions around what you want and what is best for the two of you. I could not imagine getting married without Papa at my wedding. He had always been a part of my dream, and I wanted to make that happen. So am I . . . by having a three-month engagement!

—newly engaged

Planning a short engagement can also be a protection against enormous physical temptation. A wife of three years shares:

> The hardest thing to me about the engagement was not all the stress of planning a wedding, but rather keeping our relationship pure. My husband and I were both virgins when we got married, so sex was something we had waited for in anticipation our whole lives. During the engagement period, the temptations are so great! You know that this is the person God has for you and that you will get to have sex that is right in God's eyes, so part of you is like, "Why wait?" I am so thankful that God protected us and we waited, but it took some effort on our part. During that time, it is important to be around people a lot and have close friends who are asking you tough questions to hold you accountable. If you aren't answering to anyone, it can be easy to hide your sins. Another important thing for us was to not be alone late at night as the wedding got closer. We had to say, "It's time to go home." We would sometimes joke that "nothing good ever happens after midnight." And it is true, because your hormones will be raging during that phase of life.

Engagement is a time to plan the big day. It is not a time to decide if he is truly *the one*. That decision should be made before the ring is accepted.

I was engaged for 13 weeks. It was a good amount of time for me. I didn't get my first choice of photographer, florist, etc., but it all came together and it was a nice wedding. I've got a word for you: *temptation*. Go with the short engagement.

—married six years

Engagement is an exciting time, but it can also be a time of stress. New pressures, responsibilities, people, and expectations—along with the fatigue of daily life—can get a joyful time out of perspective.

As a young girl, I always dreamed that engagement would be like fairy-tale land. Not so much. Although our engagement night was truly one of the most special nights of my life, the following seven months of engagement were tough. My husband calls engagement "the purgatory of marriage." It is a purging time, but a very good one. One of the main reasons I believe that engagement is so hard is that you are not your own family yet. You're caught between your two families, who have different views and ideas about how your wedding should be. My advice for those times when you and your family want a detail of the wedding one way, and your fiancé and his family want it another way—*keep it in perspective!* No matter what songs are played in the service or what the wedding programs turn out like, you will be married! I feel that Satan wants to distract all believers involved in weddings. He wants the focus to be turned to trivial, earthly matters. But with Christ, we are always victorious. Keep turning to Him and asking Him to keep your eyes fixed on Him, your true Bridegroom and the One who called you together and will keep you together for eternity.

—married five years

Tips:
1. Make a list of reasons for falling in love.
2. Read the list to each other during stressful times.
3. Emphasize unconditional love for each other.
4. Pray together.
5. Focus on the Lord.
6. Continue to learn more about each other.

And what if there *never* is an engagement period? What if there is a proposal and then a wedding that very night?

My boyfriend and I dated nine months before we eloped! On several occasions he had asked me to run away and marry him, but I refused. After all, I'd planned my wedding for years! My boyfriend had severe panic attacks and didn't like to be in front of large crowds. I thought he'd get over them and we could have the wedding of my dreams.

God had a different plan. On a crisp September night, I had taken my dinner break from work. As a news reporter, working 1:00–10:00 at night, dinner breaks were the only times my boyfriend and I saw each other during the week. I had recently bought a house that he was fixing up when I took our dinner there on my break. I'd not been there long when he got on his knee and asked me to marry him that very night. "I don't want to spend one more night without you as my wife," he told me. Unfortunately, I still had to do a live shot at 10:00, and since my boss watched the news every night, I had no choice but to go back to work. Meanwhile, my boyfriend called a friend (who is also a preacher), who said he would marry us, but we'd have to have a marriage license in the state of Alabama to make it legal.

Knowing my mom would know just the person to perform such a ceremony on short notice, I called her on my way back to work. Sure enough, she called the local probate judge (also her friend), who happened to have a marriage license at home that night. When I finished my news story, I called my mom, who asked me to pick a time and place where we wanted to marry that night. The probate judge was up for the challenge!

My boyfriend and I decided that midnight at my grandmother's house would be the perfect place to tie the knot. After calling our closest friends and family, we drove there—him wearing the suit he wore on our first date, I in the clothes I'd worn to work! Fortunately, all of my old formal gowns were tucked away in a closet at Gran's house! A white one, four sizes too small, hung there. I'd once worn it in the Miss Olympian pageant, then to a Phi-Delta Swap at Ole Miss! We pinned the dress so it fit (enough to walk down the aisle and say "I do"). Once everyone had driven in from Nashville, Tuscaloosa, and Huntsville, a family friend played the piano as my best friend's father walked me down the aisle to meet my mom, who gave me away to the man God so graciously created for me to love.

Our little ceremony was nothing fancy. But it was filled with 35 people who loved us and lifted us to the highest standards God wanted us to have in our daily life as one. We didn't have rings, flowers, or decor like most weddings. We had my new sister-in-law and best male friend stand by me as maid of honor and man of honor. My boyfriend's father and brother stood by him as groomsmen. My grandmother gave me the engagement ring Grand-daddy had given her many moons ago, and the ring my aunt fished out of an old jewelry box belonging to her ex-husband! Our friend who played the piano also sang "The Lord's Prayer" a capella. My bouquet and wedding cake came from a well-known discount store, and friends took hundreds of pictures.

Tears come to my eyes two years later as I remember the night that all my dreams came true. My husband is a man of God. He is the man I respect, trust, and love more deeply than I do myself. He makes me better because of his example. I am so thankful God gave us the gift to love each other. It is an amazing gift. Every day.

I have no regrets marrying the way we did. A party was held in our honor (much like a reception) where all of my favorite things I'd planned all those years became a reality—without all the fuss and tension planning a wedding brings. God

knew I couldn't handle planning a wedding well—
I would've been a "bridezilla" for sure!

Proposals come in various packages. Engagements come in all flavors and colors. But the end result is marriage. That is what it is all about.

> After becoming engaged, we made it a point to look forward to making plans for our marriage, and not just the wedding details. Our wedding was one of the most memorable days of our lives together, but the cake was eaten, the gifts were opened, and the flowers eventually died. Our marriage will last longer than that one unforgettable night. It is crucial to look at an engagement as a time of marriage planning. My husband and I were able to talk about expectations, fears, and what exactly we saw as our future together. We were realistic about issues that might arise with newly married couples, and felt prepared to work through them if we needed to. Looking past the wedding and discussing our marriage during our engagement has been a major reason why I do not feel that our newlywed period was hard.
>
> —married five years

So what do you do while being engaged?

three

Laying the Foundation

"Unless the Lord builds the house, its builders labor in vain."
—Psalm 127:1

Recent statistics report that people with loving, fulfilling, and satisfying marriages live longer, have better health, and in general have a higher satisfaction about life. In fact, people who stay married are reported to live an average of four years longer than those who don't. In contrast, divorce dramatically increases the likelihood of early death from heart attacks, strokes, hypertension, and other serious illnesses.

People long for their marriages to be successful. Libraries and bookstores are filled with marriage and relationship books. Yet reading books full of wonderful ideas about marriage does not guarantee a great marriage.

The typical bride will spend between three months to a year preparing for her wedding. Approximately 150 to 500 hours are spent looking for just the perfect dress, wedding cake, flowers, band, caterer, bridesmaid dresses, and gifts. The list goes on in the myriad, minute details that make a wedding perfect. The wedding will come and go, but the marriage should last a lifetime. The goal is to have a relationship that will go the distance.

Just as the wedding took a lot of thought and planning, the marriage itself takes a lifetime of commitment and work. Great marriages don't just happen. Foundations must be laid early on, and that begins with the engagement. It is not uncommon for a bride, with all of the pressures and preparations for the wedding day, to neglect her relationship with her fiancé. The average couple will spend ten times more time preparing for the wedding event itself than they will for their actual marriage.

So where do we begin? How can we prepare? What preparations need to be made? How can the foundation be laid properly? Investments made early on pay tremendous dividends throughout the entire marriage.

Premarital counseling can be a wonderful tool.

Some of the best advice we received during engagement was in our premarital counseling. We had a session on expectations and they encouraged us to speak openly about them. It started with simple questions like, "Who will pay the bills?"

or "Who will take out the trash?" but progressed to much bigger issues such as, "How will we split time between families?" "How will we spend our money?" and "How will we encourage one another in our faith?" These might sound obvious, but I had no idea how many unspoken, preconceived expectations I had about these areas until we started speaking about them. And, no surprise, my fiancé's expectations were often very different than mine.

Now that I'm married, I can see how valuable that session was in preventing conflict down the road. It sparked countless conversations during our engagement, when we could speak freely about the expectations we had for our marriage. We were able to make decisions and compromises while engaged that helped set the course for our marriage, rather than battling them out once we were married. Unmet expectations are such a huge source of strife, unhappiness, and disappointment. If you can express your expectations up front, and agree on what is reasonable, there's a much better chance of having those expectations met, or even exceeded, in your marriage. That has certainly been true for us!

—married three years

Many couples recognize the benefit of premarital counseling. However, most sessions compute to a total of about five hours. A diligent couple may commit to reading books about marriage. For others, the initial investment may require much more time.

My husband and I did our premarital counseling before we were engaged. He didn't want me in the middle of picking out flowers, cakes, and bridesmaid dresses while we were hashing out issues we'd face in marriage. He wanted all that done in advance, then I could focus on the wedding. That was so wise of him. So for six months before our engagement period began, we went about one time per week or two times per month, and studied a great workbook written by H. Norman Wright and Wes Roberts called *Before You Say "I Do."* We had weekly homework as it pertained to the chapter, and we got so much out of it because we were just dating! We weren't focused on the wedding, parties for us, etc. That really prepared us for marriage, and I felt that there were no surprises as a result of the in-depth six months of counseling with a great, reputable Christian counseling clinic.

—married four and a half years

This couple cared deeply about the success of their marriage. Their commitment began even before their engagement. Another couple took it a step further. Since a great marriage requires tremendous work, they decided to have checkups with their counselor.

We went through premarital counseling when we were engaged (and I highly recommend it!). After we got married, we decided to go back to same counselor every six months for a checkup. We go to the doctor every year to make sure we are physically healthy, so we thought, how much more important it is to check up on our marital health. Typically we are not having any problems when our appointments come, but the counselor has a way of bringing up issues and topics to help us strengthen and deepen our marriage.

—married three years

Some people say marriages fail because of a lack of commitment. Others would say a spiritual foundation had not been properly laid, or there is simply a lack of willingness to sacrifice. But most would agree that communication is vital. The importance of communicating freely, openly, and frequently cannot be overstated. Communication provides an opportunity to work through issues rather than just hope they will go away.

This is well illustrated by the saga of the green chest.

The Green Chest and Other Lessons on Communication

Being the thoughtful and loving fiancée that I once was, I vowed communication would be key in our marriage. We had been through the essentials of premarital counseling and knew our communication strengths and weaknesses like the backs of our hands. Well, it comes time for gifts, and my parents decide to give us a piece of furniture for our bedroom. Well, I really wanted an antique dresser. So in our typical family fashion, my parents gave me money and told me to buy what I liked. How special, right? So off I go to the furniture flea market to find the perfect piece. Nothing store-bought for us! Well, I find this fabulous green antique chest from the Czech Republic that is perfect! So

I snatch it up and bring it home. When my fiancé comes home, I have him close his eyes and give him a big surprise. Only his response to the green chest turned the surprise on me. He hated everything about it. The drawers, the color, the antique charm. He wanted functional, I wanted style and originality. So there we had it. Massive fight number one, and we weren't even married yet! Feelings were hurt, tears were shed, accusations of poorly handled money (which could lead to a whole different topic), and one-sided decisions being made. Fortunately I'm a quick learner and haven't made that mistake in the two years since. And just so you know the outcome, the green chest looks really great in our foyer. Compromise is key!

The moral of the green chest is knowing your partner, which only comes through real communication. Not only in disagreements, but in the fun times. Spending time at dinner without the TV on and with no books or magazines in front of you. Hearing the ups and downs of the day. Spending quality time with your husband and learning to communicate with him is much like spending time with the Lord. You can't just do it when you need help and things are going poorly and you need someone to listen to you vent. The joy comes in giving and receiving the love and encouragement of marriage!

Developing good communication takes a lot of time, skill, and intentional effort. How we listen, discern, and respond to information can be dramatically different from that of our spouse. Engagement is a time of learning to hear each other, but marriage will demand even more dedication on hearing what was said.

A young engaged woman has been forced into a crash course in communication because of a long-distance relationship.

Part of putting each other first has been learning how to communicate with one another. Our long-distance relationship has forced us to constantly work on communicating better. When we disagree, we talk about it on the phone and listen to each other. Avoiding the issue isn't enough; we have to talk about it until we get closure and feel at peace. The distance apart helps us learn how to encourage and comfort simply with words. His tone of voice tells me all I need to know about how he is feeling. Even though we wish that we could be together, we appreciate this time to develop our communication skills.

If communication is key, what can I learn about it?
1. Listen carefully.
2. Realize everyone interprets what they hear differently.
3. Watch for nonverbal communication.
4. Learn to hold your tongue.
5. Make time for communication.
6. Learn from miscommunication.

One of the hardest things about marriage is communication. Men do not just open up and tell you what they're feeling, how their day has been, etc. When we were first married, I talked to my mom and my friends lots on the phone, and my husband would often watch sports on TV in the evenings when I was on the phone. Sometimes we did not even talk that much to each other except during dinner. We realized that we were making each other mad with the choices we had made. I was mad that he was watching too much TV and he was mad that I was always on the phone, so we decided to change our ways. We would come home in the evening, sit on the porch or sofa and just talk, mostly about events of the day. Always ask your husband open-ended questions so you won't just get a yes or no answer! Now that five years have passed, we are effective communicators. We usually talk now once we've put our little girl to sleep and we'll catch up by chatting and end the night before we go to sleep by praying together.

—married five years

Marriage is something you have to work at every day. I once read that marriage is like a bridge, with you and your spouse on opposite sides of the river. And that you must build that bridge toward each other from scratch as each day is a new beginning. That's a lot of work; for if a day goes by and you don't work on building the bridge, then you are awfully far apart. This image has stayed with me—there's a lot of truth in it.

—married six and a half years

Yes, great marriages take a lot of work. Bridges must be built, foundations laid. Communication is key. But just what do we communicate about?

four

Let's Talk

"If you have any encouragement from being united in Christ, if any comfort from his love, if any fellowship with the Spirit, if any tenderness and compassion, then make my joy complete by being like-minded, having the same love, being one in spirit and purpose. Do nothing out of selfish ambition or vain conceit, but in humility consider others better than yourselves. Each of you should look not only to your own interests, but also to the interests of others."

—Philippians 2:1–4

Many women spend the early years of marriage working hard not to make waves in hopes the little irritations and sensitivities of their husbands will simply go away. However, this does not work. Problems not dealt with in the early years of marriage become larger and more disastrous as the years go by. One of the biggest expectations many newlyweds carry into the relationship is that their spouse will respond or react in the same way they do. Two very imperfect people have committed themselves to each other. No couple marries being completely compatible. Therefore, there will be conflict and it must be dealt with on a daily basis. Freedom and growth in a relationship take place as husband and wife begin to be honest and open about their feelings, thoughts, dreams, and expectations. This will happen only in a safe, unhurried, and comfortable place. Sharing on the deepest level is possible only if the spouse feels loved and free from judgment.

I feel that I never was truly able to be comfortable with myself around people until I met my husband. It was then that I realized someone could love me for being myself, flaws and insecurities and all. That is one of the things that I love the most about being married. I am accepted, cherished, and appreciated for being the unique woman that I am.

I am proud to be called a wife. I am also a daughter, sister, granddaughter, mother, and friend, but the title of wife holds a high significance to me. One week after we were married, my husband introduced me as his wife to a colleague. What went through my mind at that point was pure joy. God truly blessed me when He created the man that He chose as my husband. I feel honored that my husband saw something in me that made him want to open up and share his dreams and ambitions.

—married five years

Hurts and concerns should be expressed rather than keeping everything bottled up. This does not, however, give license to become harsh or hurtful. Choose words wisely and remember to be slow to speak rather than quick to respond. Talking about an issue before it becomes charged with emotion and anger is important.

My husband and I always say we are a team, and it is so true. When one person is having a hard time, the other is there to lift spirits, take over, and then the roles will be swapped. We each do our part in making the marriage run smoothly. I cook and he cleans the dishes. When we do chores, I clean the bathroom and he'll vacuum, etc. It is always a team effort for us, but takes a great deal of communication and a lot of forgiveness and unconditional love along the way, too! It is amazing that just last week we celebrated our fifth anniversary! It has flown by, but we feel so graciously blessed being happily married with a beautiful daughter, who is two, and another baby due July 11. God is so good!

—married five years

Learning to work as a team takes a lot of time and effort. Honesty is key if you're really going to communicate and share what you're thinking and feeling. Likes, dislikes, hopes, dreams, hurts, and disappointments can affect your relationship if honesty is not paramount. The smallest miscommunication can lead to unresolved conflict.

The hardest thing we dealt with when we were first married was resolving our conflicts quickly and not "letting the sun go down on our anger" (Ephesians 4:26). When you are dating, you can go home or just get away from the other person and stew over something for a while before you resolve it. When you are living with the person, it is totally different. You can't get away from them, so you have to deal with it. I remember our first major fight was over spaghetti sauce, of all things. (I grew up eating ready-made pasta sauce and his mom always made the sauce! I had never even heard of his mom's cooking before we got married and then all of a sudden for every meal, he would say, "Call my mom. She has a great recipe." I now respond, "I have a great recipe also!") Anyway, we were so annoyed with each other and we sat down to eat. I was furious because I knew I had to pray with him to bless the meal and I knew I couldn't with the way my heart was at that moment. Needless to say, we had to deal with what we were feeling before we even ate one bite of our meal. You really have to be quick to talk and resolve issues before they fester or else marriage will be no fun. And that conviction stems from being connected with the Lord so that He can prick your conscience and let you know when your heart is not right.

—married three years

Marriage is a process of learning and growing together as one. Changes must be made in the transition from being a single person to being married. Patterns and habits must change as new ones are established. Awareness that lasting change will take time can free a wife or husband from resorting to negative nagging to motivate change. Instead of nagging, try praying. God has the ability to take a heart of stone and turn it into flesh (Ezekiel 11:19). Again, coming together as one takes time, but it is worth the effort.

> When we married, I adored my husband, respected him immensely, trusted him completely, and loved him with everything I had. And everything I felt that day, I feel ten times as strongly now. However, I thought, if we had love, what else would we need? The first two years were a learning period, about each other as separate entities and about us together as one. It wasn't until the third year that we started to work as a team more smoothly, and it wasn't until our second child (four years of marriage, but I think it was more due to the second child) that we really came together to think and function as two parts of one that are the head of the family. That was an amazing transformation.
>
> —married six years

Conflicts arise over many issues—one of the greatest is dealing with money.

Marriage is absolutely wonderful. Being able to see your husband and best friend every day and every night no matter what is amazing. Even if my husband has to work late, I know that he will be home sometime that night. It gives me such a great feeling inside to know that I will see him each and every day.

Although marriage is a ton of fun, it is definitely hard at times. The hardest thing that we have had to deal with in our marriage is money. Both of us were fortunate enough to grow up in a family that was not struggling or pressed for money; however, our views on money are entirely different. My husband is extremely frugal, and I am more on the spending side. The number one issue in our marriage is how we should spend/save our money. It is a constant battle, and we've only been married less than a year. We are both working on understanding each other's views and coming to a happy medium, and we know that the longer we are married, the more natural it will be to, in my case, save more money and, in his case, spend a little more.

—married less than one year

Attitudes toward money and the use of it can be completely different. Many couples come into marriage with a lot of money of their own. They haven't had to think about it. Since people are waiting longer to get married, well-established professions along with wise investments have placed people in their 20s at a higher economic level than that of generations past. So what do we do? How do we handle our money?

One newly married women wrote, "Separate two things: checking accounts and bathrooms!" That is fine for some, but impractical for others.

Another woman, married for two years, wrote:

Biggest hurdle: finances! Even though my husband and I are blessed in abundance by God financially, we argue about how we should spend it. A great way to avoid this conflict is to discuss finances and financial goals in your premarital counseling. We saw a counselor for about eight to ten sessions before we married and that was the best thing we could have done to prepare us for obstacles. Map out a budget monthly, yearly, and five years from now to help one another plan for expenses. This will allow you to not be surprised when a $2,000 hunting trip shows up on your credit card bill.

Questions to ask yourselves are:
1. Am I a saver?
2. Am I a spender?
3. What does money mean to me?
4. How do I want to spend it?
5. What motivates me concerning money?

In God's economy, everything—and that includes money—belongs to Him. He wants to provide for all our needs. We are to be stewards of what He has entrusted to us. As our hands are held open, freedom from the control of money is released.

Budgets, spending limits, savings, and planning are decisions that need to be talked about. One of the best ways to get on track financially is through tithing. God delights in proving His faithfulness to those who give Him the "firstfruits" (Proverbs 3:9) of what is earned.

As in all facets of living, dying to self becomes key to establishing a wonderful marriage based on a strong foundation. A wife of two years shares her thoughts:

> The biggest adjustment for me as a newlywed was recognizing my own selfishness. Imagine all the little preference clashes you had with your college roommates, then multiply that by ten! I quickly learned that giving of myself completely to another person requires just that, giving. Whether it is little disputes about what is the right way to fold a bath towel and what to eat for dinner, or bigger challenges like budgeting our finances, I have to constantly keep myself in check. I need daily reminding that it is not about *me* and my wants, it is about *us* as a marital unit. It is essential to our marriage that we make decisions together, in unity, not as two independents reaching a compromise. The most important element of our decision-making process is praying together. When we pray together, I feel an incomparable intimacy with my husband. It is only then that we are able to really act as one cohesive unit.

A newly engaged woman shared that her fiancé's 82-year-old grandmother told her that the key to a great marriage is always putting the other person first—one of the central truths of Ephesians. Her marriage of 60 years serves as an example to this soon-to-be-married young couple. Sacrificial loving and serving, even in difficult times, creates a marriage that goes the distance.

How wise to listen to older generations and also learn from and about your spouse's family. After saying "I do," you not only become a part of your husband's life but also a part of his family. Their traditions, expectations, and values may be completely different from yours. Again, it is important to remember that relationships take time to form.

A wife of six years writes:

Be kind with regard to his parents. Work to understand them, because that is a large part of how he works. And they are not just his parents—they will one day be the grandparents of your children. Remember that when people of different geographical states marry, there are quite often strong cultural differences that we don't realize because we are still in the same country. So remember they will do things differently from the way perhaps that you were raised—expect this and don't be surprised that they don't do things just like your parents did. Be open to change and new things and ideas. The only thing we really fought about that first year were in matters of extended family—and it was me, being hard on his parents and family because they were so extremely different than mine. You are marrying their family too—no matter what you might think. Be sure you love them. If his mother does not treat you well, it is your husband's job to stand up for you.

And, on a practical note:

Always respect and be kind to your in-laws. Remember that before your husband got married, his mother was the leading lady in his life. It is great to do little things to let her know that she is still important and loved greatly. I try to call my mother-in-law every now and then just to talk. I like to let her know what's going on in our life and keep her in the loop. Sometimes guys aren't so good at picking up the phone, so it's a good way to include her and let her know that she is loved.

—married two years

Communication is key to a healthy marriage. It is a lifelong process and takes commitment, love, and patience. A six-year wife concludes with her set of principles to live by.

1. Never go to bed angry.
2. Never assume your husband has any idea what you want—always spell it out!
3. If something is important to your husband, it should be important to you.
4. Always be open and honest—don't lie even about little things.
5. Trust your husband.
6. Always tell him you love him and how great he is.
7. Find a good church and a Sunday School class with couples your age.

Marriage is a process—a growing process—but what makes it so difficult? A popular book says it's like we're from different planets. Just what are those differences?

five

Vive la Difference!

"The LORD God said, 'It is not good for man to live alone. I will make a helper suitable for him.'"

—Genesis 2:18

In the beginning of creation, there was man. His life was filled with a beautiful, perfect garden, which he tended and enjoyed. There were plants to name and animals also, but God saw that man was lonely. He was incomplete.

"So the LORD God caused the man to fall into a deep sleep; and while he was sleeping, he took one of the man's ribs and closed the place with flesh. Then the LORD God made a woman from

the rib he had taken out of the man and he brought her to the man. The man said, 'This is now bone of my bones and flesh of my flesh; she shall be called "woman," for she was taken out of the man.'"

—Genesis 2:21–23

God created a helper suitable for Adam. Eve was a complement to him, which meant she was distinctly different from him. This was God's plan. So why is it so difficult for men to understand women and women to understand men? The fact of the matter is this: Men and women are wired differently. And that begins with basic needs.

A husband's needs may include:
1. Sexual fulfillment
2. Recreational companionship
3. Admiration
4. An attractive wife
5. A pleasing home

A wife's needs may include:
1. Affection
2. Talking and listening
3. Honesty and openness
4. Security
5. Strong family unit

Most men want to be their wife's hero. A man is affirmed when allowed to be the person of strength—to be the protector and provider. However, many women today feel that when they acknowledge and accept the differences in the roles of men and women in marriage, they become less equal. Equality, however, was established by God at the beginning of creation.

"Then God said, 'Let us make man in our image, in our like-ness.' . . . So God created man in his own image, in the image of God he created him; male and female he created them."
—Genesis 1:26, 27

No one responds well to someone who demands power and control. However, in a godly marriage, the key ingredient is service and giving to each other. In making a husband the hero and giving him his strength, the wife's needs are met as his life becomes open and is gladly laid down for his bride.

A lot of women are becoming like men. This is dangerous because men will often retaliate against an overbearing woman by having an affair. A man will go where his strength is acknowledged and he is admired. The emotional and spiritual consequences of mixed-up roles can lead to physical separation. An affair is much more about power, control, and separation than it is about sex. The strengths of men and women are very different. They are designed by God and should be honored and respected.

God's prescription for marriage stands in stark contrast to the way of the world. And this type of marriage requires effort on the part of both husband and wife.

I don't want it to sound like marriage isn't wonderful, because it is, but painting a rosy picture won't really help anyone. Marriage is great, but it is work. Every aspect of it is work. It is wonderful to have that confidant and best friend with you most of the time. It is wonderful to raise children together and to know another person so intimately. It is wonderful to make and fulfill dreams together. I just think that knowing up front that things won't always be perfect is better than going into marriage with a fairy-tale mentality. If you do that, you will most likely always be disappointed.

I just think so many people go into marriage thinking that if it doesn't work, then they will just get a divorce. People expect marriage to be like the love stories that they see in the movies, but it isn't that way all the time, and people really need to know that before they tie the knot. It is rewarding, but anything worth getting is worth working for, and marriage is no different.

—married six years

Women would rather have their needs met than live in a palace. As a wife responds correctly to her husband's needs, he will respond with gentleness and protection. If a husband approaches his wife with honor, respect, dignity, affection, and true romance, she is designed by God to respond enthusiastically. God's plan really works.

"Submit to one another out of reverence for Christ."
—Ephesians 5:21

Here's what I know now: you *must* have respect. And do little things to take care of one another. Bring him coffee in the mornings. Have dinner waiting on him when he gets home. And always work to see things through his eyes, stand in his shoes—even in an argument. And just because he does it differently, it doesn't mean it is wrong. It's just different from the way you do it. And you might learn something from the way he does it.

—married six years

God designed man and woman as complements to each other, but He never intended for even the intimacy of marriage to fill the place that was meant for Him alone. As Christ fills us, we are better able to meet the needs of our spouse. A wife of six years writes:

People always say that a husband and wife are supposed to meet each other's needs—as if the person God chose for you will be able to complete you. I think this leads to a lot of disappointment in marriages, and a selfish outlook as well.

While it is true that God has chosen someone who is perfect for you, who will complement you, and who can show you a picture of the best you can be, the goal should not be for your husband to be the one to complete you.

If we allow the Lord to be the One to fulfill and sustain us, the One who is our refuge and strength, we allow our husbands to be the ones to be our companions, friends, and the ones whom we walk with on our journey without demanding that they meet all our needs. Our outlook should be about serving our spouse and looking at our relationship as a gift. I have found I can only do this when I am relying on God to be my everything. I have learned this the hard way!

Another woman agrees:

> It is important to put God first, and then all things work together much better in your marriage. If we are putting Him first in our lives, then we are able to truly serve one another. I once heard someone say, "Marry the guy who serves you the most." That is what I did. I married a servant with the heart of Jesus Christ and God has blessed me indeed. I have the challenge of trying to serve him to the degree he serves me and our child.
>
> —married four and a half years

A young woman who has been married three years admits she is still learning that God must remain her first priority even with a loving, attentive husband.

> Marriage has been one of the greatest blessings in my life thus far. It threw me into a whole new season of life to learn and grow. What I love most about it is that it feels safe. I know at the end of the day, my husband is always coming home to me—to love me and support me. On the flip side, though, that has been one of the hardest things. Because my husband is tangible, it makes it easier for me to rely on him and turn to him before I turn to God. I know that God has given him to me as a confidant and to encourage me in my walk, but God must still remain my number one priority. It is something I have to preach to myself day in and day out. It is so easy to just get comfortable with life and being a wife and put God on the back burner. Thankfully, God is gracious when I repeatedly fail to learn my lesson.

No one human being will ever be able to meet all the needs of another. That was never God's intention. Men and women are different. And in many cases, girlfriends understand best. Be sure to include them in your life after marriage.

> Don't expect your husband to be like your best girlfriend. Men don't have the same amount of emotional energy as women. It is unfair to expect your husband to be everything for you. Yes, he *can* be your best friend, but remember he is a man. He does not have the same needs for relating as you do. Remember that all your needs are met first in Jesus and then you can have a wonderful fulfilling relationship with your spouse.
>
> —married two years

Developing a spiritual life in your new oneness will knit the union securely. Yet, connecting spiritually as a couple on a consistent basis can be a challenge.

Where do I begin?

six

Spiritual Unity

"Let the peace of Christ rule in your hearts, since as members of one body you were called to peace. And be thankful. Let the word of Christ dwell in you richly as you teach and admonish one another with all wisdom, and as you sing psalms, hymns and spiritual songs with gratitude in your hearts to God."

—Colossians 3:15–16

Connecting spiritually on a consistent basis is often more challenging than most couples anticipate.

Single life affords time for Bible reading and prayer. It is easy to set a regular time and place to meet with God.

Mornings are quiet and predictable. But what happens when God is not the only one to wake up with? When there is a warm, wonderful, huggable husband waking up with you? How does God fit into the picture? How can you make sure that He is still first in your life? An important fact to remember—you will never be able to love a spouse as God calls you to love him, unless you seek God first.

There will be days when it is easy to love your spouse. The world is rosy, with love filling the air. However, it is certain that on other days loving may seem impossible. It is on those days or during those seasons of life when loyalty to God gives couples the heart to stay together, even when they don't care for each other and staying together is the last thing they feel like doing.

A wife of six years recounts the advice her mother gave her before she married.

My mom once told me something when I was dating my husband: You will not always feel like you love your husband. During those times, remember your commitment. To take it a little further—remember your commitment to yourself, each other, those family and friends in attendance at your wedding, but especially to God. Of course, this idea of commitment must be believed in by both parties. You cannot remain in a marriage if the other person refuses. Make sure your fiancé believes marriage is a done deal. Dating is as close as you should come to dress rehearsal. Once you're married, the show is on!

Commitment to the marriage is key. In drawing close to God, husband and wife draw closer to each other.

Intimacy is often built when focused on a third object. People who work together on projects, serve in the military, or play on sports teams tend to bond because of that on which they are focused. This is sometimes called by theologians the "transcendent third."

A married couple may focus on children, houses, and professions—only building their lives together. These things may bring them closer to each other, but will never bring about true spiritual connection. There must be a husband and a wife seeking God individually to bring them together in their spiritual journey as one.

When love isn't felt, it is that loyalty to God that stabilizes and covers all other loyalties. Christ gives the proper perspective, and this can lead to change. God's Word is truth and His truth sets us free, even in the midst of mutual annoyance.

Personal quiet times with God are crucial, but also important is a time set aside in which to grow together as a couple. This is not always easy for a number of reasons. Spiritual unity does not mean spiritual uniformity. The husband and wife may have come from completely different denominations. Worship styles may be different as well as structure of services. You might feel you are on completely different wavelengths, and the truth of the matter is, you just might be. Don't let this catch you off guard, but remember that the goal is to grow together spiritually and this may take time.

A wife of two years made an important step in this direction before being married.

My husband was raised in one denomination, and he is very devout. He never misses church on Sunday, and even when he is out of town he finds a church to attend. I was raised in a different denomination, but as our relationship began to deepen, he asked me to start thinking and praying about possibly changing denominations. I did, and God showed me through prayer and the Word how important it is to worship as a family. My family was very supportive as I took this journey, which helped tremendously.

Changing denominations was a big commitment. I went to class every Thursday night for nine months. My husband and I both became much stronger Christians, and God used this experience as a springboard for our relationship to grow stronger in Him. As I sit in church on Sundays with my husband and my son, I thank Him for leading us together. My husband and I fully participate in the service together, and we are raising our son in the same faith. We are a team, with God at the head. I can't imagine not attending church together and worshipping with each other. Because we share the same faith, I feel like I can come closer to being the godly wife the Lord intended me to be. There is a closeness that I cannot put into words when we worship together. The Holy Spirit is there, and we both feel His presence. What an amazing gift!

Another wife shares:

The best thing that we have done for our spiritual relationship is to get involved in a Sunday School class together. Getting to know other couples at our church has been such a great experience for us. It helps to be able to worship and study the Bible with other couples and makes you feel like a part of the church. I feel that it has helped to build a strong foundation for our relationship. It also holds you accountable for making it a priority to be at church on Sundays.

—married two years

There are many spiritual disciplines that can be shared as a couple.
1. Prayer
2. Bible reading
3. Devotional books
4. Memorizing Scripture
5. Listening to sermons
6. Worship music

You may want to start small by choosing one spiritual practice to do regularly as a couple. The key is to plan something that is doable and do it regularly. There is no right and wrong way. Here are examples:

Pray for and with your spouse daily. Pray specifically. For example, pray for better communication. Pray for an intimate sex life. Pray for your future children to the third and fourth generations, pray for your spouse at work, pray for financial wisdom and your budget, pray that God will intertwine your hearts more and more. Read the Word together, for it is your plumb line, the standard for your marriage. Share at the end of each work day. We often say our "high" and "low" of the day. Make sure you take time at the end of a long day to share.

Also, preach the gospel to one another. It's not about trying harder to accomplish something. It's about needing Jesus. My husband and I have a "State of the Marriage Address" almost every month. It's the time we share with one another one way we think the other has grown and one area we think he or she needs to grow in. It's hard to hear the negative, but we are to be each other's accountability partner and to build one another up. It also prevents us from having to constantly bring up negative things because we know we'll have our address each month. However, communication is key. So if something is really bothering you and is creating a burden, talk about it on that day. Don't let it build up. A mentor of mine told me in my first year of marriage something that's been very valuable. She said, "Share with your spouse openly and honestly what is on your heart, even if you know it's a selfish thought. If you don't, it festers and causes tension." Don't hide anything from each other.

—married five years

As two people draw close to God individually, their relationship with each other will strengthen. Spiritual intimacy with God knits hearts together. And those committed hearts show the world what God's love is all about.

> You may have heard that you need to set your expectations low when it comes to changing your husband, but I think it is more correct to say that you should have the *right* expectations for your husband, meaning that you always look for the good, Christlike qualities in him and draw them out over the course of your entire marriage (and pray that he would do the same for you). You should hope for and expect to see spiritual growth and change in each other. Sometimes drawing these qualities out requires encouraging words, actions, sometimes a gentle reminder; but most of all pray that the Father would change you both to be more like Him, and that the difference would be seen not only by each other, but by the world, to the glory of God!
>
> —married five years

OK, you have met the guy of your dreams. You've fallen in love, have the ring, have gone to counseling, and are now starting to plan the wedding. Just how much advice have you been given? Let's hear some.

seven

A Smorgasbord of Advice

"*Finally, brothers, whatever is true, whatever is noble, whatever is right, whatever is pure, whatever is lovely, whatever is admirable—if anything is excellent or praiseworthy—think about such things.*"

—Philippians 4:8

It is a fact that as soon as word begins to spread with the excitement of a new engagement, ideas and advice become abundant. Decisions are being made. Invitations are being ordered. The guest list is being compiled. Parties are being planned. And the lists of "to-dos" goes on and on and on. Before you know it, the wedding has taken on a life of its own. It is out of control, gaining more and more momentum as the hours and days progress. As a result, many young couples approach their wedding day—one of the most important days of their lives—totally exhausted physically, mentally, and spiritually as well. What can be done to prevent this?

A young lawyer purposed that his engagement would be both well planned and guarded. He, along with his fiancée, devised a plan that has yielded a very fruitful, sane, and meaningful engagement. His plan follows:

1. Start premarital counseling immediately after becoming engaged. The arguing/listening skills and training would have been helpful prior to the stress of the engagement.

2. Close yourself off from the world with your fiancée for the last month of the engagement. Don't plan anything with other couples; learn to establish boundaries during that time. This helps to focus your time on getting the wedding tasks done and not wearing yourself out trying to keep a busy social schedule.

3. Try not to talk about your wedding with anyone. This is difficult. Shift the topic of conversation to the other person's life. Otherwise, all conversations tend to focus on you, and it is easy to become self-absorbed.

4. Pray together with your fiancée regularly. Learn to pray together and learn to pray for specifics— pray for your wedding service (that the Spirit would be present and the enemy bound); pray for your family relationships; pray for purity; and pray to keep Christ at the center of your relationship.

5. Learn to identify the attacks of the enemy. These will become more prevalent as he is upset that two believers are coming together. Call on the Holy Spirit to protect you and your fiancée, and tell Satan to get behind you! (Matthew 16:23; Mark 8:33)

6. Have fun! Get excited about getting married. Let yourself daydream about being married. It's an exciting time in your life!

7. Keep all your love letters/emails from before your marriage. Mesh them with your fiancée's letters and make a scrapbook. Someday your grandchildren will enjoy reading about your courtship. (This will also keep you accountable regarding some of the issues you can discuss with your fiancée via email.)

8. Try to remember to exercise and eat well especially during the last month of the engagement. During the last month it is easy (and necessary) to plan something to check off the list every few days. It becomes too simple to skip eating, sleeping, and exercising.

9. Don't cop out and take anti-anxiety medicine (if necessary) during the tough times of the engagement. Learn to cope with your spouse and learn to pray together. I think that God condenses innumerable relationship issues into the short period of your engagement. You can either use them as a catalyst to strengthen your relationship, or you can numb yourself, only to have those same issues resurface later.

A plan of this detail obviously requires tremendous discipline of both the man and the woman. However, this 28-year-old man takes his own responsibility to a higher level as he makes a final point intended for the man.

> Divorce and affairs are so prevalent now. Make your relationship that much more sacred by saving the blessing of physical intimacy for your marriage. Be the leader of your relationship and keep the relationship pure. Don't do anything more than kiss and hug your fiancée during the engagement.
>
> It's so tough—especially when you are tired and at your fiancée's house late at night and you don't want to drive home. Resist the temptation! Remember that Satan tempted Jesus after He was weak from fasting. Don't let yourself get attacked—get up off the sofa; go home before 9:30 P.M.; don't undress while your fiancée is in the same room; don't split hotel room beds on trips; etc.
>
> Know that you cannot do this without God's grace. Call on God's protection and the assistance of the Spirit to put on the armor of Christ.
>
> "It will be worth it on your wedding day to look at your wife coming down the aisle and knowing that God is pleased with your conduct."

A wife of two years gives a warning for engaged couples:

> Understand that when you get married, it is inappropriate to form new relationships with members of the opposite sex. Likewise, it is not OK to spend time alone hanging out with someone of the opposite

sex. If your mate has a feeling about a guy who hangs around the two of you, trust him and honor his wishes. Men can often detect signals in other men to which we may be blind. Simultaneously, your husband should also follow this guideline, and if you get a weird vibe about another female, he should accommodate your wishes as well. Remember, most all affairs begin as benign friendships.

Having a husband for a best friend is one of life's greatest blessings.

The best thing about being married is living with your best friend. My husband and I are both attorneys. We both work very hard and are usually exhausted when we get home at the end of the day and get our baby fed and asleep. But it is usually on those days when all I want to do is get in a hot bath and go to bed, something happens and I am reminded of how lucky I am to have the man I adore, the man God prepared for me, to talk to, listen to, and be quiet with. That something can be as little as a wink or a squeeze of the shoulder from my husband. It is the little, simple things in marriage that make it so wonderful!

—married two years

My favorite thing about being married is that you have a built-in best friend. This, of course, only counts if your mate is indeed your favorite person in the world with whom to spend time. Remember being young and always having to ask if your best friend could come along on trips and to gatherings? Well, the great thing about marriage is that *everyone* knows and understands that your best friend will be included in plans, and if they don't like it, tough turkey.

Best friends are great, but a husband is a little different from relationships with girlfriends. He doesn't leave when it is time to go to sleep. And that means he is there on good days and bad also.

Time and time again, I have heard the comment, "If only we were married!" Most of the time this comment is in reference to a fight between a couple. "If only we were married, it would be so much easier to work things out" or "If only we were married, he wouldn't be able to run away from the relationship." However, my one piece of advice would be to realize that when you get married, fights are that much harder. No matter what the disagreement or how strongly you feel about your point, you must come to an agreement. There is no running away once you're married. Instead of disagreeing and fighting, you must remember that you are on the same team, and that you must work together. It may seem easy to think that you won't be fighting about dumb things when you get married, but believe me, just because you're married does not mean that the little fights end.

The best advice I can give someone is to make sure you really know the person that you're going to marry. Know that person's strengths and weaknesses. Prepare yourself because you do not want any surprises to come after you're married. Fortunately, I dated my husband for five years before we got married, so I haven't had too many surprises.

—married two years

A newlywed wife shares a lesson she learned from her pastor:

One of the best pieces of advice we were given came from my pastor, who married us. It's called the "four-minute rule." It goes like this: for the first four minutes after one of us comes home from the day, we are to greet each other and give each other words of affirmation, etc. If either of us has a bone to pick or if we need to share some bad news, we try our best to wait until those four minutes are up before saying anything. Trust me, the conversation will go much more smoothly and you really begin to look forward to coming home!

Little irritations can become huge wars unless properly dealt with. A married couple of three years spoke of difficulties in marriage:

Learning how to divide chores—who does the dishes can become a sore subject very quickly. My husband and I worked out a plan: I load the dishwasher and he unloads. It's worked out pretty well for the last three years. Also, learning to pick one's battles is a difficult task. There are some things that just aren't worth getting upset about. One must learn how to talk openly, honestly, and often. Both parties must be willing to say what's bugging them *when* it's bugging them. Letting rage simmer until explosion is a surefire way to ensure future divorce. And when my husband and I have disagreements, we make every attempt to remember what it is we're trying to get from the confrontation. If what you want is a return to a loving and caring relationship, then yelling and denying affection isn't going to get you the results you want.

Balancing life, marriage, and a profession can be tricky, as this young wife of two years—who is a lawyer married to a lawyer—writes:

> For me, one of the hardest things about married life was the realization that I was not going to be Donna Reed (or even anywhere close). As much as I try, I cannot do it all. I cannot work outside the home and cook five meals a week. I cannot take care of all the errands and have a perfectly neat and clean home. I know it sounds ridiculous that I thought I could do it all, and even as I write I am smiling, but I thought that it was possible. Not only possible, I expected it out of myself (my sweet husband would never put that type of pressure on me). I thought that was what a wife did. I was wrong. A wife takes care of her family. And a wife cannot take care of her family if she does not take

care of herself. To be a good wife and mother, I need to have my quiet time; I need to exercise; I need to use my brain; I need to be with friends; and I need to have dates with my husband. I do not need to have a stocked refrigerator ready to prepare dinner; I do not need to always look perfect; I do not need to be on every volunteer committee; and I certainly do not need to be Donna Reed! When you become a wife, you are still *you*. Your husband loves you for the person you were before you said your vows. The ring on your finger doesn't change that. Stay true to yourself!

A smorgasbord is laden with all types of food. Not to be neglected is the best of all—dessert!

Be spontaneous and silly, because marriage is supposed to be fun! Realize that as you get married, your identity is changing. I felt that I had to die to my little girl self and become my husband's wife. It's hard to let go of your maiden name sometimes because that is who you've been for your whole life. But marriage is a mysterious adventure of "two becoming one." Your identity is in Jesus, anyway. You are His precious child. Rest in His love for you!

Laugh often and laugh long. Now is the time to plan the wedding day.

"I Do"

eight

"O, LORD, you are my God; I will exalt you and praise your name, for in perfect faithfulness you have done marvelous things, things planned long ago."

—Isaiah 25:1

This is the big moment—one of the most special and memorable experiences two people will ever share. Many couples will want the wedding ceremony to be steeped in tradition, to convey the importance of this step, while being filled with elements unique to the personalities of the bride and groom. Wedding ceremonies are as varied as the imagination allows, and they express values, family ties, personal preferences, and lifestyles. Most importantly, the wedding itself should be a joyous celebration of the wonder of two people becoming one.

A newly engaged young woman plans for her big day.

Three months ago, I entered the euphoric period we call engagement with a sparkling new diamond on my hand and a smile that wouldn't leave my face. With six months to plan, I plunged right into designing the big day that I had dreamt about since childhood. I soon found that coordinating a wedding can be time-consuming, overwhelming, and even a bit stressful—not quite like the fairy tale I had concocted as a little girl. With so many choices and decisions to be made, I wondered if eloping was not such a bad idea after all! Throughout the planning process, however, I have unveiled a few strategies to keep the stress level low.

Here are her tips for planning a stress-free wedding:

1. Stay organized! Organization is a key ingredient, particularly if you are not working with a wedding coordinator. Use a calendar or wedding planner to write down details, contact information, dates, etc. If you keep all brochures, business cards, invoices, and other important documents together, it will be much easier to find what you need when you need it.
2. Make a priority list. Whether working on a tight budget or handling various opinions, making decisions can be stressful. If you make a priority list, you will be able to determine where to place the majority of your budget or where to stand strong when conflicting opinions are thrown your way.

3. Be open-minded. When making decisions, you will suddenly find yourself inundated with more opinions than you could ask for. Relatives, in particular, may have strong opinions on certain aspects of the ceremony or reception. While it *is* your day, be open to suggestions from others. This will ease some tension and eliminate some arguments, as well as make those close to you feel important and involved during this special time in your life.

4. Do research. Thousands of books have been written to address the various questions and needs of brides. To ensure that your wedding day turns out as you envision, select several books to gain ideas and tips so you can clearly communicate your ideas to vendors. If you have something specific in mind, take pictures if possible, particularly when selecting a wedding dress or flowers. Research will also help you learn what foods, flowers, or colors are in or out of season at the time of your wedding, thus helping you make decisions that save you money and work with your budget.

5. Appoint a shower/party coordinator. Select a bridesmaid or friend to be the official contact person for showers and parties. As friends volunteer to host a party, refer them to this person, who will coordinate hostesses, dates, and party themes. This will allow you to focus on other details of the wedding rather than becoming consumed with planning showers.

This young woman emphasizes the importance of staying focused on the marriage itself rather than getting caught up in being queen for a day.

I absolutely cringe every time I hear people talk about how a bride should be queen for a day. That self-centered attitude permeates our culture in magazines, TV shows like *Bridezillas*, and the endless companies that market their products to engaged couples. It seems accepted, even encouraged, for modern brides to have a "me! me! me!" attitude. Reality check: *It's not about you.* It is about your marriage, you and your fiancé together, your families joining, all of your dear friends who have watched you grow, and most importantly, it is about the Lord. It is easy to become self-centered when you are the bride; don't let that happen. Remember this is something much bigger than you looking gorgeous, making a grand entrance, having the prettiest flowers, and bigger than having the best band at your reception. This is a sacrament, a holy joining of two people, an event your parents and grandparents have probably been praying for your entire life. Looking beautiful and having a great celebration are not bad things, but they can become bad when they are the main focus of your attention and efforts. I encourage you to focus on the special people you share this time with, not on the things that distract us from what marriage is all about.

—married two years

A wedding takes place in as little as an hour, but marriage should last a lifetime. With this in mind, many of the crises, stresses, and disagreements that come with planning a wedding become completely inconsequential.

A wife of two years reflects back to her wedding day:

> I would advise keeping the wedding simple. It is only one day and poof, it's gone. I was so worked up over whether or not my guests were having fun at the reception that I couldn't enjoy it myself. If I could do it all over again, I would have a private ceremony on a tropical island (maybe just close family) and then have a casual reception when I got home. I felt so guilty about how much my family spent on the wedding that I never enjoyed it. There are a lot more responsible things you can do with the money your parents give you for a wedding!

Planning a wedding can be very time-consuming, and the event itself can be extremely costly. A young bride-to-be, along with her fiancé, knew they would need to be creative and resourceful to have the perfect wedding at a reasonable cost, as the mother of the bride was not only a widow but a schoolteacher. "We were not able to put on an extravagant wedding for me," the young woman remarks.

This plan took time. In fact, it began even before the couple officially became engaged and lasted about one year from the actual wedding date. A lot of research and legwork went into this wedding of frugality.

1. A wedding dress was found that cost at least one-third less than the original price.

2. Family and the bridal party, along with the bride, put together all the flowers. Many wholesale florists sell fresh flowers to the public. The cooling room at the florist shop may also be rented for storage after the flowers have been arranged. Bridesmaids, flower girls, and the bride each made their own bouquet. This allowed each to be creative and have a lot of fun together at the same time.

3. Having the wedding and the reception at the same place can be cost effective. This bride chose to get married at the church and have a reception at another place. However, she chose a caterer to do all the food, drink, and cakes.

4. Photography is often one of the most expensive parts of the wedding. A photographer was found outside of the city without big city prices.

5. Borrow, borrow, borrow—lingerie, veil, even shoes.

6. Get married on a holiday, when the church is already decorated. Very little will need to be added.

7. Buy decorations on sale and cut back on fresh flowers. (They are going to die anyway!)

8. Hostess presents can be very meaningful if a donation is made to a charity in honor of each person who has helped to give a party.

9. This bride let each bridesmaid choose her own long black dress so they were not forced to spend a lot of money on a dress they would not wear again.
10. Make your own programs and save-the-date cards. Using postcards also saves money on postage.
11. Collect change! Over six months, this bride saved more than $300. Pennies, nickels, dimes, and quarters can add up.
12. Make personalized bridesmaids gifts. Get crafty with photographs, oil painting, and books.
13. Recruit friends and family who offer to help decorate for the rehearsal dinner and reception.
14. Wear family jewelry rather than buying something new.

This very resourceful bride concludes with this thought:

The best thing about planning this wedding was working with my fiancé. At first, he said he did not care much about decorations, flowers, etc. But the more I talked about it, the more input he had. This way, you can do it together and the wedding day won't only be about you, but about both of you!

Weddings take a lot of planning, but often those plans become useless when outside circumstances change everything. Such is the case of a young bride and groom who had their wedding turn into a tremendous adventure as Hurricane Ivan became an uninvited guest.

As most girls do, I had dreamed of my wedding day forever. In fact, my mother and I had already planned parts of my wedding and its events even before I ever had a serious boyfriend. Being from the South, my wedding was planned around two very important things—the weather and college football. My dreams included an outdoor reception in my parents' backyard, which meant setting a date well before mid-April or after September. Being outside during summer months can be brutal in Florida—especially in wedding attire.

October 9, 2004, was set as the wedding day. Everything was going as planned—the church, music, photographer, cakes, band, caterer, reserved hotel rooms, flowers, tents, bride's dress, and bridesmaids' dresses. The days were in countdown mode as even scale drawings were made of the backyard and all the reception areas . . . from the mashed potato bar to the Plexiglas-covered swimming pool as the dance floor. The bride and her bridesmaids had gone to New York City for their bachelorette weekend.

The girls and I were interviewed on the *Today Show*. All the regular hosts were there, except for Al Roker, who was on location in Florida, with all of the hurricane action and predictions for Ivan.

Three weeks before the wedding, Hurricane Ivan hit Gulf Breeze and surrounding areas as a Category 3 storm, tearing up much of the Gulf Coast.

Pensacola Beach and Gulf Breeze were disaster zones. Suddenly, my wedding didn't seem important. Thank You, God, my parents' home was fine, except for missing shingles, a few downed trees, tons of yard debris, and our boat stuck up in the roof of our boathouse!

The wedding details became more numerous. Power was out and there was a lot of devastation in every direction. The wedding dress had been left at the downtown shop, awaiting alterations and final pressing. Two sides of the building were gone, with about 75 percent of the inventory either hanging from trees or soaked in mud and seawater. Amazingly, the owner had taken this bride's dress to her home to work on. It was safe!

There were now three weeks to handle three big challenges:

1. Hotel rooms—all had been either destroyed or taken to allow for emergency workers.
2. Rehearsal dinner—planned for a restaurant on the beach, which had been damaged.
3. Departure from the reception—friends had planned a getaway on their beautiful boat, which now sat crushed beneath a stack of other boats while in dry storage.

The challenges were met:

1. About 20 (very random) hotel rooms, spread out, in and around Pensacola, were found and reserved.
2. Close friends welcomed bridal attendants into their homes and neighbors on either side of the bride's parents' home relinquished all their bedrooms for out-of-town family members.

3. The bride's parents volunteered their backyard for the rehearsal dinner and arranged for the reception caterer to also prepare food for the rehearsal party.
4. A limousine was used instead of a boat for the departure.

The bride reflects:

As we continued to prepare and clean our yard and house, in the back of my mind stayed the thought of many close friends who had lost everything in the storm, including their homes. We took a wedding planning break and helped with cleaning their yards and homes, even cleaning mud and seawater out of kitchen cabinets! We also spent some time passing out water at distribution sites, and serving meals to out-of-town Coast Guard workers at our church.

The wedding day arrived, along with reports of impending rain as another tropical storm loomed in the Gulf of Mexico. The storm did not hit until after the wedding, when the bride and groom were safe in their hotel room.

As the bride's father remarked at the reception, "A 'man' kept trying to destroy this couple and their wedding, but to no avail." Ivan was, of course, that man.

The wedding day will come and there may or may not be surprises. But there comes a time to stop planning and just enjoy this important day—the wedding.

By nature, I am a planner/thinker/analyzer/organizer/ doer. The months leading up to my wedding were no exception; in fact, they probably brought out the best and worst in my personality. About six weeks before my wedding, a good friend sent me a gift certificate for a 45-minute massage. I decided to schedule it for late afternoon on Thursday before my Saturday wedding. Once it was scheduled, I marked it in my mind as the stopping point. I knew all planning, rearranging, worrying, etc., had to be done by 5:00 P.M. on that Thursday because I wanted to enjoy my wedding weekend and enter it relaxed. And you know what? It worked! Set a specific time when the planning will stop and the fun will begin, and stick to it.

—married three years

And once the wedding begins, be all there, as this bride of five years encourages:

Marvel at God's sovereignty and goodness in bringing two souls together, formed to be "one before time." *Pray* that God will enable you to exalt and worship Him, whether or not the details of the wedding unfold as you had planned. It's not about the wedding details, but the wedding vows. *Laugh* at the things that go goofy that day. My husband and I got all mixed up when the preacher was guiding us through the vows. The congregation laughed with us. *Pray* that God will enable you and your mate to taste of your heavenly Bridegroom's wedding banquet. *Look* into your spouse's eyes the entire way down the aisle. Don't look left or right, but straight into your soul mate's eyes. And realize that one day, as you go to be with Jesus at the eternal wedding, Jesus's and your eyes will be locked forever. *Pray* with your wedding party before heading into the church. Hold hands and invite Jesus to be the center of the whole service. *Pray* that you will soak it all in. The whole day is dreamy; yet there is probably not another time in your whole life when you'll have all the people you love most and who are interested in your life in the same location. Ask God to supernaturally allow you to have still, full, and aware moments. Be all there and glorify your maker. And *dance* at your reception! Have a *blast* at your own party.

And when all is said and done, don't forget to be thankful.

At our wedding we created special notes for people to receive as they entered the reception. My fiancé and I spent many hours the month before the wedding writing personal, handwritten notes to each of our guests (yes, all 250 of them!). The purpose of the notes was to thank each guest for celebrating with us, and to let them know what a blessing they had been in our life. We tried to include something personal, like a special memory or lesson we had learned from them. As people entered the reception, each guest received the little envelope with their name on it. I just loved the fact that people were expecting to get just a table assignment, but instead they received a note of appreciation.

—married three years

The day after our wedding, my husband and I felt so overwhelmed with gratitude for all of the people that made our wedding so wonderful for us. Of course our parents, but friends as well. While we relaxed and soaked in the excitement of our wedding weekend, family friends were hard at work being sure that everything was perfect for us. My former kindergarten teacher was at my reception site long before I was, making sure that everything was like I would want it. Another family friend strung lights and greenery around my outdoor tent because she knew I would like it. I think it's so important to remember and thank everyone that helped in any way with your wedding. They obviously love and care for you very much!

—married three years

nine

Reflections
and Gifts

"A longing fulfilled is sweet to the soul."

—Proverbs 13:19

The wedding day has come and gone. All the months and maybe even years of planning, dreaming, and working for that very day come to an end. There's a good chance you're feeling a bit blue. Or maybe you just feel a little let down. Now is time to reflect on that day.

Several brides look back at what went wrong with their wedding.

The one major thing that went wrong with my wedding was with the invitations. We had someone else address and stamp them for us and she was going to mail them as well. So my mom delivered all the invitations to her and brought the stamps. (I was studying for the bar exam, so my mom helped out a lot.) Well, to make a long story short, we did not think to have the entire invitation weighed and we did not have enough postage on the invitations. Praise God that the post office called my mom and held all the invitations in boxes for us to pick up, restamp, and get back to the post office. It was very stressful because we had to go through the invitations list and make sure that we had gotten every last one. You know, people gripe and moan about government employees, but that one employee at the post office went above and beyond. I am just glad that I had angels watching out over us or it would have been a disaster with all the invitations mailed back and stamped *Insufficient Postage*—we would have had to start over!

The bridesmaid dresses that came in three weeks before the wedding were the wrong ones. The right ones did not come in until the day *before* the wedding. We got them altered and ready to go the morning before the rehearsal dinner.

The cake was supposed to be a beautiful, classy Wedgwood green color, but it came out turquoise! No big deal, though.

When my wedding party went to pick up the flower arrangements from the rehearsal dinner to transport them to the wedding site the next day, they had been picked bare by the country club staff! Be sure that all involved know what's going to happen to those flowers!

While some brides see what went wrong, other are thankful for choices made concerning their wedding day.

People always say that you won't remember anything about your wedding. On the way to the wedding, I stopped at the reception place. I walked around and looked at all of the flowers and decorations and soaked it all in so that I could remember how it all looked and felt. I was so glad I did that because the reception was a whirlwind!

—married two years

Our wedding day was such a day of joy and celebration! We both just smiled through the whole day and loved every minute of our special day. We really focused on what we were saying to each other and remembered it later on. (Many people say it is a blur, but it doesn't have to be.) We chose to see each other and have all our pictures taken before the wedding. At first, I was opposed to this idea since I am more of a traditionalist, but now it is some of the best advice we were given, and I recommend it to other brides too. My husband and I had a few (5–10) minutes together alone to see each other before the photos started. Before I saw him, I was nervous, but when I saw him and for the rest of the day, I was much calmer and just very happy! We were so pleased that after the wedding we could walk directly to the reception (held at the church) and we were the first ones at our own party. It was fun to greet everyone and not arrive 45 minutes later after quickly trying to do all the wedding and family pictures.

—married two years

We did "releasing the pews" at our wedding, and it was wonderful! It's done a lot out west. After we were pronounced husband and wife and walked out of the auditorium, we had our pastor announce that we were going to come back in (we also had it printed in the program). We came back in after all the wedding party had left and went from row to row releasing each pew and alternating sides. It was great how everyone waited and were all so excited to see us. We liked it because we didn't have to have a receiving line at the reception; and since we had shuttles taking all the guests to the reception and they all couldn't get on in one trip, it gave them something to do besides wait by the side of the road. The pictures from this are awesome!

—married one year

Important details to you may not be as important to your groom. Keep in mind that men would often rather look at the big picture as opposed to the minute details. They may not care what your wedding cake will look like or about the flowers you use. The type of wedding invitation you choose or the wording you use on it may be meaningless to your future husband. When you register for wedding gifts, often a fork is a fork to your fiancé. He may not care what type of cereal bowl he eats out of or what type of linens you will use on your bed. Don't take this the wrong way. Your fiancé just may not want to be bogged down with details. This has nothing to do with his love for you. Think of it this way: You may pick out the beautiful things you love, and you will know your future husband will love all of them.

—married one year

My father not only walked me down the aisle, but he also performed the ceremony (he's a Presbyterian minister). It was deeply meaningful to me when, at the end of the ceremony, he put his hands on the shoulders of my husband and me and issued the benediction I'd heard him give every Sunday of my life growing up, "And now may the Lord bless you and keep you . . ."

The wedding party actually faced the congregation, and the pastor (my father) was seen from the back. It was delightful to see my friends and loved ones, and they loved seeing us as we took our vows.

The church in which we were married was nearly 150 years old and was a setting for the movie *Big Fish* (we didn't know that until the movie was released). Our reception site, Marengo Plantation, was featured in Kathryn Tucker Windham's *Thirteen Alabama Ghosts and Jeffrey.*

—married two years

Weddings mean gifts. Lots and lots of gifts are given as well as received. Some brides recall their favorite wedding gifts.

Our favorite wedding gifts came mostly from family members—artwork, furniture, and family heirloom silver pieces. We love antiques, so any unique gifts were very special, and I treasure my silver flatware because we actually use ours every day instead of only on special occasions.

My favorite wedding gift was from my husband's sister and brother-in-law. They gave us their frequent flyer miles. Since we were paying for the honeymoon ourselves, this made things much more manageable.

Favorite wedding gift: gift certificates! That is all I give for wedding gifts now because it was my favorite. You really don't know what you need until you merge both your belongings together. In my case, I moved into my husband's house after we married. I had to clean out a lot of his stuff just to make room for mine. If you combine that with a bunch of wedding gifts that you have no use for, it makes for a lot of chaos. I ended up taking almost all my gifts back for store credit. Once I had our house organized, I then went back to purchase things with that credit a little at a time. This way I made sure that we had everything that we needed, not just useless stuff.

Registered items—especially my china. Bedside tables and lamps that we really needed. I found that if you really want something, just tell people what you want or where you're registered. It helps them just as much as it makes you happy.

The Briarcliff Shop, a favorite for special wedding gifts, has shared their top ten list of gifts for the bride-to-be:
1. Lamps
2. Elias picture frames
3. One-of-a-kind silver serving pieces
4. Monogrammed linens
5. Silver tray
6. Artwork
7. Crystal candlesticks
8. Wooden boxes
9. Furniture (side table, end table, etc.)
10. Cookbooks, antique books, and/or coffee table books.

A wife of two years prepares her own special wedding gift—a gift that keeps on giving.

As recent college graduates, the expense of going to and being a part of all our friends' weddings can be burdensome. We certainly can't afford to buy our friends a place setting of their fine china or silver! My favorite wedding gift to give to new brides is a "newlywed cookbook." I love to cook, so I compiled about 100 of my favorite recipes from my two years of marriage. As a new wife, I would much rather try recipes that I know a friend has recommended than pull something random from a cookbook. This gift costs very little, and all my friends have really appreciated their cookbooks. I just print the recipes on pretty paper and put them in a three-ring binder with a sweet note. It does take time to type them all up, but the beauty of it is, once you have them in your computer, you can simply reprint them for endless more wedding gifts.

And what about gifts for bridesmaids and hostesses? Here are a few ideas:

I am giving my bridesmaids the perfect shoes to wear in my wedding. After they bear the expense of their dresses, I would hate to give them an additional cost like shoes. I do want all of them to be matching in the wedding, so I decided to find the perfect pair of shoes and give a pair to each of my bridesmaids in addition to another gift or two.

I have found a wonderful hostess gift for those who throw any type of event for my wedding. Well in advance of the event, my mom has found an opportunity to take a picture of the hostess and me. We have framed the picture in a beautiful silver frame. By the time the event rolls around, I already have a great photograph in a beautiful frame to present to the hostess as a thank-you.

I was in a wedding a couple of years ago and the bride gave all of her bridesmaids a monogrammed bag. This was a great gift. The bride knew all of the bridesmaids would have hairbrushes and makeup and other items to primp with prior to the wedding; but once we walked down the aisle, all of our belongings would still be sitting in the church dressing room. So, we packed all of our things in these new cute bags. The bride arranged for someone to pick up our bags and take them to the reception. We did not have to worry about them, and neither did the bride.

Gifts are as varied as those who give them. Weddings, too, have the charm and personality of the bride and groom involved. But marriage should be permanent . . . "for better or worse, for richer or poorer, in sickness and in health—till death do us part."

And marriage begins with the honeymoon.

ten

The Honeymoon Begins

"For this reason a man will leave his father and mother and be united to his wife, and they will become one flesh."

—Genesis 2:24

Weddings are incredible events. Marriage, on the other hand, is much more than an occasion. The wedding vow "till death do us part" denotes permanency—a union meant to go the distance. A relationship meant to last a lifetime. The success of a marriage, however, begins long before the "I do's" are said.

As the organ majestically sounded "Lift High the Cross," bridesmaids and groomsmen processed down the very long aisle of a beautiful old downtown cathedral. The candles glowed as evening light streamed through intricate and glorious stained glass windows. The bridegroom stood straight and tall, in full military dress, eagerly watching for his beautiful bride to appear.

Everything about this wedding was as perfect as could be. As for the marriage itself, a foundation had been building for almost a decade. While in junior high, this beautiful bride had been given a purity ring by her dad. He held his daughter to God's highest standards and was careful in helping to guard her heart. This dad spent a lot of time with this groom as communications were opened and intentions declared.

While the congregation stood, all eyes looking intently toward the back of the cathedral, the bride, adorned in white, walked quietly on her dad's arm. The ceremony had been planned carefully. The music timed perfectly. Yet a most wonderful and unscripted moment occurred—known only to father and daughter. Before reaching the aisle that led to the altar, this young bride gently removed her purity ring: "Here, Dad." He later remarked, "I almost lost it."

Several weeks later, this new wife flew home alone to return wedding gifts and pack with and direct movers. Proudly she showed her new driver's license bearing her new married name. Her grandfather quietly remarked to the new bride's father, "You sent her off as a girl. She's come home a woman."

And that is the way it should be. A man leaves his father and mother and begins a new life with his wife. That begins with the honeymoon. This time is certain to be filled with adventures and awkwardness as two people embark on the journey to oneness.

A wife of three years shares:

> Since we were both virgins when we got married, we didn't know what to expect on the honeymoon. The one thing I learned is that sex is nothing like the movies! It can be really awkward and uncomfortable. It is also hard to mentally make the transition that it is now OK to be naked in front of each other. My advice is to just laugh together. Be thankful that you have a lifetime together to work on it, and don't stress if it doesn't go as planned.

A newly married wife shares:

> I would say that the most important thing you need to have on your honeymoon is a sense of humor. We arrived in Costa Rica on the Sunday after our wedding, tired, but nevertheless excited about the week ahead. I had all of these thoughts about what a honeymoon would be like, but one certainly didn't cross my mind. I knew there would be fishing, ATVing, eating, beaching . . . and a king-size bed.
>
> Only problem was, the travel agent forgot to let the place know that we were honeymooners. We arrived at our attractive little villa only to find two twin beds.
>
> We looked at each other in dismay while the Costa Rican was unloading our luggage, and we knew we were in for it. Because my husband is more than six feet tall and on the bigger side of guys, I knew I would have a week full of my own

bed. That is exactly what happened. He called his mom one night and said, "Yes, I am just lying here watching TV, with my blushing bride across the room in her own bed." The beds were cemented into the ground and could not be moved.

It really was quite comical.

A wife of three years shares a very practical piece of advice concerning honeymoons:

The best piece of honeymoon advice we received for our Saturday night wedding was to leave for our trip on *Monday* morning instead of *Sunday* morning. We were exhausted upon leaving our reception Saturday night. It was so nice to arrive at the hotel that evening knowing we had no agenda except to enjoy being husband and wife. We slept in Sunday morning, had a late breakfast, slept most of the afternoon, and were rested and excited to hit the airport Monday morning for our flight. I can only imagine the stress and exhaustion of an early Sunday morning wake-up call following a Saturday night wedding. Plus, on a financial note, it was much less expensive to spend Sunday night at a local hotel than it would have been to spend that same night at our honeymoon resort.

Even better advice:

Don't forget to pray over your honeymoon. So many young women get wrapped up praying about the wedding and all the details, they neglect to pray over their honeymoon. It can be such a sweet time of fellowship, de-stressing from the wedding, etc., but I have heard some horror stories—and girls said they wished they had prayed more over their honeymoon week with their spouse.

Marriage is hard work. And that work includes time spent in the bedroom.

I honestly thought something was wrong with me when I was able to think about something other than sex in the first few weeks of marriage. As far as my experience is concerned, those movie newlyweds were unreal. There's a lot more to early marriage than sex, and it may take a long time (I'm talking as long as a year here) for you to be fully comfortable in this area. So just relax and have fun.

—married four years

Weddings can be comical when disasters occur.

Finally we were pronounced husband and wife; my sister picked up my veil to give it one final fluff before we headed down the aisle. At the same time, my husband was so excited that he bolted, causing my veil to fly out of my hair. The congregation roared with laughter as my sister tried to wrap the cathedral-length mass of tulle around her arm. Consequently, my husband's first words to me on video after were married were, "Did you just trip?" As my sister was escorted out, she decided to pass off the ball of netting to my mom, but during the handoff it got tangled and she was forced to take it back. The whole thing was so humorous that we even sent our wedding video back to have the scene added to it.

Honeymoons can also be filled with the unexpected. But of utmost importance is the realization that the goal is to have a solid, loving marriage. Two imperfect people becoming one must start with the deliberate attitude to *make* things happen and not just *let* things happen.

Unfortunately, I believe most women are brought up with the wrong ideas about sex. Before I got married, I taught abstinence education to middle school and high school kids, and the questions they had blew me away. Most all of them knew way too much about all the wrong things and not enough (if any!) of the right things!

The world lies to us about sex and love because it doesn't know the One who created love and sex. Women (married or not) have a craving for love deep within them. We were created like this for a reason! Our longings are so strong, though, that they cannot be met by anything on this earth. Only our heavenly Father can provide us with that unconditional, unending love we all desire. That being said, we do still long for love on this earth, and we should. God wants us to love one another. But we search in the wrong ways . . . some women seek perfect friendships to hold them up; some women seek attention from young men, which leads to horrible mistakes and regrets later on. Some women spend their lives searching for Mr. Right to fulfill all their longings for attention and love. And even though marriage is God's design, He didn't design it to completely fulfill us. Instead, we should view love and sex as God's gifts to us within the protection of marriage.

As a wife, it is my privilege to know my husband intimately, and sex is an expression of that knowledge. And just as we grow in our knowledge of who our husbands are over time, we also learn more about our sexual relationship over time. So instead of the world's view that sex is only exciting and fun with strangers, we should know and believe that only in a marriage are we allowed to experience the fullness of God's design for sex, and it will only get better as our marriage grows and our love deepens for one another. That being said, sexual union is not always a number one priority for women. We tend to feel close to our husbands simply by sharing a deep conversation or cuddling up on the couch! But we must remember how men are designed.

Satan has many temptations and traps set for the men we love, and it is a *huge* part of our job as a wife to fulfill our roles as our husband's lover, so that he will not be led astray or tempted to look for that fulfillment (whether he means to or not) in something or someone else. So, I recommend marking your calendars (I am not kidding!) to see how often you have sex. Do not let too much time pass. Try to be realistic and set goals with your husband about his versus your expectations and try to keep those goals. (There will be seasons of life where this is hard to do, but don't let it slide.) Sure, you may not always be in the mood, and it may not always be the best, but it is crucial for a healthy marriage! Above all, *pray* that God would purify your marriage, that your love and desire for your husband would be true to His design. And pray that God would protect you from all temptation. I don't believe wives can ever understand the struggles our husbands have: They are up against a world of lies, images, music, and emotions that we must be aware of. You cannot pray enough for your husband's protection!

—married four years

Marriage should be wonderful—a lifetime of loving and getting to know another person. But marriage and a husband will never fulfill all your needs. It wasn't designed to do this!

"Look to the Lord and his strength; seek his face always."
—1 Chronicles 16:11

And sometimes waiting a long time for your mate may be God's good plan for your life.

eleven

God's Timetable

> "*There is a time for everything, and a season for every activity under heaven.*"
>
> —Ecclesiastes 3:1

Marriage was designed by God. It is His good plan for mankind. In times past, the majority of men and women married while very young. In modern times, the norm has changed drastically. Many couples wait until their late 20s or early 30s to marry, while others choose to marry at a much later age.

I would like for all women to know that it is OK to wait for the person God has chosen for them. I was older when I married and am so thankful that I never settled just because many of my friends were marrying. There were many lonely times, but it was worth the wait to marry the person God had planned for me many years prior to my marriage. My husband and I were college sweethearts. But after graduating, we both went our separate ways and did not marry until many years later.

This woman recounts the fact that while they were in college, the idea of marriage scared her now husband. She continues:

I encourage women (of all ages) to wait for the person God has planned for you. Please seek God's guidance and much-needed patience for waiting. Marriage is a wonderful gift from God, but being married to the wrong man can cause more pain than the pain of loneliness. Do not try to make things happen with someone. It just does not work. When you marry the person God has planned for you, making things work is just not necessary. I personally wasted so much time trying to make things happen with the wrong people.

—married three years

A beautiful, talented, and very successful woman in her 50s was asked to be on a panel for the career single women's ministry at a church. The young women could ask anything, but the panel was told to expect several questions on dating and marriage. As she introduced herself, and as it stated in her bio that she had married for the first time shortly after turning 47, she imagined that she could hear them silently praying, "Lord, please don't make me like her!" But in reflecting on her life experiences with dating and marrying while preparing for that panel, she could see God's sovereign, loving, and protective hand on her life the entire time. "The process He put me through could not be hurried, even though I tried," she recalls. Her advice—practical and spiritual—should be of encouragement to those still waiting.

1. Spend time with God. Don't just do it so you can check it off your list, but spend time with Him as you do with your friends—talk to Him through prayer, listen to what He says as He speaks to you through His Word, and give Him large blocks of unhurried time. I've spent hours in the Psalms, seeing and feeling the emotions of the writer and realizing I could be just as intimate with God as he was. In fact, one of the most helpful studies I did was called *Intimacy with God* by Cynthia Heald. For the first time in my life (by this time I was in my 40s), I began to feel God could fill that ache and hole in my heart that I thought only a husband could fill. I remember a thought coming across my mind, *I think I could really enjoy my life if it's God's will for me to be single*, and that was something I had never felt before. God knew I needed to learn to let Him fill my deepest needs because that is something a husband cannot and should not try to do.

2. Have realistic expectations of marriage. I am guilty of having what I would call the Cinderella Syndrome—expecting a fairy-tale existence of

loving and being loved, and continuation of the romance experienced in the dating relationship. The romance and love can still be there, but what about coming home from work to a hungry husband who is wondering what is for dinner, clothes that need to be washed or ironed, and a bathroom growing cultures in it that need your attention. All of a sudden, I felt there was no time for myself, only enough time to go to work and then tend to things around the house. Both my long quiet times with the Lord and time spent reading the newspaper and books were all gone! Only now, five years later, am I learning how to find that time for myself.

3. Don't put off improving yourself or your circum-stances because you think you may marry soon. Take courses you are interested in, whether or not they are related to your career. I enjoyed taking tennis lessons and even Cajun dance lessons, and getting to know others through the church who liked the same things. Seminary courses also challenged me and helped me know and understand God even more. Discover what you like to do and find others who like to do it too! Buy a house if you can—I finally was able to at 40—and it proved to be a good invest-ment. Learn to live within your means and how to save money.

4. I can't say enough about having strong convic-tions in your life that are grounded in Scripture. This would even include places you will or will not go with girlfriends, as well as guys. Stay

above reproach! I found it helpful while dating one guy to be accountable to a friend. She could ask me anything about what had happened on the date and I had to tell her. Be ready to explain to a guy why you won't have sex with him—I remember having to do this twice, both times with guys I had met at functions for singles at my church. And if you think it is impossible to wait until marriage to have sex, from the mouth of one who waited until 47, *it is not!*

5. Learn to wait on the Lord. He never said it would be easy; in fact, He said it would take courage. Memorize this: "I would have despaired unless I had believed that I would see the goodness of the Lord in the land of the living. Wait for the Lord; be strong, and let your heart take courage; yes, wait for the Lord" (Psalm 27:13–14 NASB).

Life is fragile. Life is short. Never to be wasted by just filling in time until marriage comes along.

An older wife of four years writes:

Few things terrify a man more than the feeling that the woman he is getting to know is just waiting to pounce and lead him to the altar. Certainly you may want marriage. It may be on your mind—but not all the time, and not with every man you meet and date. Let a good friendship mature. If more is meant to come of a relationship, God will let the man in on the idea. There is no reason to scheme. Pray over the relationship, asking God to orchestrate it. Relax. When you meet someone, try thinking of him as a human being with hopes, fears, and aspirations of his own. Leave yourself out of the picture for a while and watch his life. See what his character is all about. Stop. Watch and listen.

A recently married woman of 48 emphasized this fact: "He is not at all what I thought my husband would be like."

What if we entertain a specific idea of what our husband or our marriage will look like? What if God has totally different yet wonderful ideas?

J

twelve

It's a
Small World

"The Lord does not look at the things man looks at. Man looks at the outward appearance, but the Lord looks at the heart."
—1 Samuel 16:7

The world as we know it in the twenty-first century becomes increasingly smaller and more connected by the Internet, cell phones, email, and massive fleets of jet planes. A hundred years ago, young people would more than likely have married someone from their own hometown or maybe a nearby city or state. Family ties were strong and multiple generations chose to live in close proximity to each other. Thus friends of families often encouraged their sons and daughters to marry each other, causing family circles to become even more tightly wound and connected.

In today's society, that is simply not the case. America, the great melting pot, is increasingly becoming more and more beige-colored, rather than stark red, yellow, black, or white. Couples marry interracially. And, countries also are being brought together through the unions of husbands and wives.

How does this work? What are the benefits? What are the drawbacks? How should obstacles be faced?

> Opposites attract. As trite as this sounds, in my case this can't be more true. The thing that you find intriguing can also be the thing that irritates you the most later. Just like the differences you had with a roommate in college, there will be adjustments in living with your husband. Someone will always be cleaner than the other. Perhaps you'll marry a morning person and you're a night person; or, you might be an introvert and your husband is an extrovert. And the list goes on and on. Recognize these differences and work together at a compromise. Communication is key! You don't want resentment built up over a toothpaste cap.
>
> —married three years

Communication can take on many forms, as a new bride from Romania shares: "At the beginning of our relationship, we could only get around at times by pointing. And even when we speak the same language, we still speak different languages." She goes on to describe the many barriers that come by bringing such diverse backgrounds to the union.

1. We have different understandings of actions and definitions of things.
2. In my country he is the baby; in his, I am the one who needs to be taken care of, be explained to, have things done for me, etc.
3. Our friends are diverse, coming from both cultures. Mediation is necessary with co-nationals in general.
4. We have different needs that are often hard to understand because of cultural differences.
5. In my country we don't talk about certain things; he asks about them up front. (The joke is that Romanians talk about money and not sex, while Americans talk about sex but not money.)
6. The things each of us have to have are often different.
7. Different eating habits—exotic foods, lots of spices, variety, carefully following a recipe, and looking for the right ingredients versus improvising.
8. Doing things that are perceived as rude or inappropriate in one's culture and embarrassing the other person is just inevitable.

This couple chose to marry in the bride's hometown in northern Romania, in a wonderful fourteenth-century painted church. The service was long, full of rituals and religious songs. But before being married in the church, they had already been married in a civil ceremony by the state officials, which is required by law. A friend served as the certified translator at the civil ceremony.

After a three-month honeymoon that covered most of southeast Asia, the couple moved to the United States.

The bride reflects:

A whole new world of varieties and possibilities open up to you when you marry a person from another culture and country. It is an experience that enriches your life a lot and gives you multiple chances to learn, to appreciate new and different things, people, and different ways, and also the possibility to choose and combine things that you like or that suit you from two different cultures.

The other's world consists of different and sometimes really new manners, customs and traditions, foods and ingredients, eating habits, different games and expressions, different symbols, approaches, analogies, history and politics, ways of thinking and interpreting things, life routine and daily life coordination, skills, attitudes, looking at a situation from a different angle. Everything is different, which requires patience on the sides of both husband and wife.

Marrying someone who speaks a different language and lives in a foreign country requires learning to bridge obstacles. But what if the bride and groom are from different racial backgrounds?

First, it is important to know that when my husband and I started dating, it never occurred to me that I was in an interracial relationship. It never occurred to my parents either, but everything changed when we got engaged. I suppose no one paid much attention to us until we got engaged. That is when we began facing a lot of judgment. Most comments were made to my parents from their peers. One person said, "What is wrong with a white boy?" Someone else said, "That would never happen in my house."

Her parents had not anticipated any of what was being said. Instead of defending them, the couple's parents began to question whether their children should marry. For months they argued and fought because they thought the young couple would be treated disrespectfully, and their children would be looked at differently. The bride continues:

Of course I didn't handle it well. I did a lot of yelling about how they should worry less about what other people think and how they should quit being so superficial. After many heated arguments, we got down to the real issues. Without realizing it themselves, my parents had a picture of what they thought my future family would be like. They envisioned grandchildren who would look like them or others in their family, and now that was less likely. It was as if they had to grieve over the fact that things wouldn't be as they had imagined. Once they began to realize that God had a different plan, a better plan, they began to come out of the darkness. We have all learned a lot. I had to be very patient with parents who were raised in a time when races were rarely integrated. Though that is not an excuse, they had to be deprogrammed. My parents learned to stand up for what they knew was right, in spite of what everyone else was saying. We all learned that it was most important to worry about what God thought and whether He approved of our union. If He approved, we could move forward and leave the comments of others behind. I can only imagine that as Christians we will make many choices in our lives that are not popular to many of our peers.

I love my life and the excitement that another culture has brought to me and my family. My world has been opened and enriched because of what my husband and his family have brought to me.

—married four years

Another wife of five years shares:

There are many different perspectives on interracial marriages (especially in the South) and unfortunately, I believe we are all missing out on the big picture of God's kingdom when we focus too much on our own expectations for ourselves and for our children. If we all took a minute to think about it, I am sure that most, if not all of us expect to marry someone who is of the same race . . . someone who looks like us and will most likely bless us with children who look just like us. I certainly believed this before I met my husband. But once I fell in love with him, for who he was in Christ, for his spiritual leadership and for his godly expectations of me, those childish thoughts were forgotten. We must be open to what God has for us, and for our children one day. Are our racial upbringings (whether or not voiced openly in your family) hindering us from accepting others and seeing them as equals in the vastly diverse kingdom of God? Sure, God may have called you to marry someone of the same race; He does so for many, many people. But are you open to accept the mates God has for your children, regardless of the way they look on the outside? We know that we should pray for a godly husband, and for godly mates for our children, but don't forget to pray that your expectations will be correct and that God will open your eyes to see all of His children as equal and worthy of the kingdom through their faith in Christ.

Marriage is hard work in any case, but when God has brought two people together, the blessings are meant to be full.

Remember to approach your life as a married person with an attitude of thankfulness for the Lord's provisions and blessings. Remember to approach your spouse with an attitude of thankfulness for the Lord's provisions and blessings.

—newly married

thirteen

For God
and Country

*"Let us therefore make every effort to do what leads to peace
and to mutual edification."*

—Romans 14:19

The people of the United States are deeply indebted to
those men and women who, since the birth of this nation,
have been willing to give up their very lives for the pursuit of liberty—for our very freedom. Along with those
who actually *go* to battle or leave their homes for military
service, military wives and the families of those who serve
make a tremendous sacrifice.

Every time the President speaks and thanks the military families for their sacrifices, suddenly he is thanking me. Though I am shaken when I stop to realize the extent to which my husband is willing to sacrifice for this country, I know that I am not the first woman to be torn between a sacrificial love that gives everything to help others and a self-ish but precious love for her husband. This struggle may reveal my egocentricity, but at least my sense of duty is putting up a good fight, and it is in this struggle where I have found strength. It is this struggle that has changed my views on everything. How differently I now see history and my place in the world through this view of a frightened army wife; what a different life I feel obliged to lead when I realize how many people's lives it has cost to provide me with all I have.

This young wife and her husband were married only weeks after his return from Iraq. Three months after the engagement, he was deployed and assigned as a leader of a rifle platoon in an infantry battalion. In other words, he did not have a safe job in Fallujah.

While her fiancé was deployed, this 23-year-old woman worked as a news producer and anchor. While many wives choose to completely tune out all media coverage of the war, this woman's personal computer included international Associated Press wire service.

I remember every single morning being terrified to turn on my computer and learn what had happened while I was sleeping in America and another day had gone by in Iraq. I remember the feeling of panic and fear every time the bright yellow "breaking news" bar would light up at the bottom of my screen, announcing the death of another US soldier. I would be in agony until follow-up reports were filed, clarifying the division to which the soldier belonged. I remember the unbelievable relief after learning it was not a 10th Mountain Division soldier, followed only by the sick feeling of guilt, knowing that at the same time I was experiencing a reprieve, another family was about to learn that their nightmare had materialized.

The deployment was presented as "the most painful and most frightening episode of my life." However, this newly engaged woman cannot think of another time when she grew more in her relationship with Christ. Before her fiancé left and throughout the first few weeks of deployment, she comforted herself with Scripture that reinforced God's protection and God's love, anything that would help convince her of God's love for her fiancé and His protection over him in Iraq.

But as the weeks went on and soldiers continued to die, I found it more and more difficult to take comfort in that logic. God loved these men and He loved their families, but still they had been killed. Finally, exhausted from constant worry and sadness, I gave to God what He had been trying for months to get from me. I handed my plans over to Him. Of course I continued to pray that the Lord would protect my fiancé and keep him safe, but I finally said that if that was *not* in God's plans, I would not curse God, but would accept it and would continue to love God and to trust Him with my life.

The moment she finally acknowledged the possibility that the Lord's plans may be different from her own, everything changed. She was still terrified because she loved her fiancé and desperately wanted him to remain safe.

But at the same time, I felt such an overwhelming peace in knowing that God had already determined the outcome. God had already made His plans for my life and for his. Our job was only to trust that His plans were the perfect will for our lives, that even if we were to end up facing what appeared to be devastating, it would have been God's will.

This young soldier arrived home safely, but with countless stories of near misses and miraculous close calls, all of which he attributes to God hearing the prayers of those who prayed for him and his platoon.

Another wife shares what she has learned after ten years of marriage as a military wife:

Wow, what a decade! It seems so long ago that I was a newlywed—naive, dependent, and clueless to what really constitutes a crisis. At the time, I thought I had a handle on what a godly marriage was supposed to look like. I had read about the Proverbs 31 wife, and I looked forward to serving my husband and children like the women of the

Bible. I knew I was not supposed to look to my spouse for my self-worth, joy, or happiness, and I even prayed a prayer in college that I would never be dependent on my husband for my emotional or spiritual well-being, only relying on our Lord and Savior for everything. You have to be careful what you pray for . . . little did I know, almost ten years later, I would be stripped of my husband for 16 months so that I could walk the talk I had been claiming for so long.

She continues:

When I married my husband, I knew that he had a strong commitment to serving our country. About a year and a half into our marriage he graduated from college and was sent to Officer Basic Course on an army post out in the middle of nowhere. This was my first taste of military life. It was also the place where God revealed to me my husband's gift and calling as a soldier. At the end of his schooling I encouraged him to enlist in active duty service, but he did not want to live the military life because he had moved so many times as a child. He thought the army reserves would be a happy medium and a good way to fulfill his desire to be a soldier without compromising our family's unity. We had long talks about his goals and expectations of his military career. I specifically remember one night when he brought up deployments. He had already volunteered in the first Gulf War in his early 20s, before I knew him, and he explained to me how peace could not be achieved in the Middle East if Saddam Hussein was still in power. We agreed that night he could volunteer for any military deployment until we had children. After that he would have to be called up involuntarily if the army wanted him to be activated again. At the time, all of this was so sterile and matter-of-fact. In hindsight, I now believe my husband had a sixth sense then that he would be going back to the Gulf sooner rather than later because of all the human rights atrocities he witnessed the first time.

At first this man became a weekend warrior, which did not affect the marriage too much. In fact, this young wife enjoyed those weekends as a time to work on projects or spend time with girlfriends. But after September 11, 2001, occurred, she saw a change in her husband as well as in the country. He would just sit, glued to cable news channels, feeling helpless as he watched reruns of people jumping out of the World Trade Center towers.

"You know we will have to do something about this," he said. Her husband had a strong sense that this was not just a war about politics but a war of ideology and principles, which, if not confronted, would compromise the future safety and religious freedom of our grandchildren and their children.

Meanwhile, we continued on with life, renovating our home, and a year later conceived our second child. It would be December before we would hear rumblings of deployments, and then in January of 2003, he got the call. All possible emotions flooded my being. Was God's grace enough to sustain me through my husband's deployment? Was Christ enough to help me through a pregnancy and then care for a newborn by myself? Did I have what it takes to be a single mom to a very active little boy? Needless to say, God showed up big-time. He showed me the power of love, family, community, and what the body of Christ is supposed to look like. God protected us at every corner. From my husband's assignment to my doctors, from family to friends, we could see His mighty hand everywhere.

God used this time of deployment to reveal Himself in such powerful ways. Some are:

1. God is sovereign (even down to your flight number).
2. God is sufficient (even when you don't know if your husband is alive and you can't talk to him for weeks at a time).
3. God gives you supernatural grace when you really need it.
4. God uses us during trials to show others His Son.
5. For those who give God the glory, Satan will attack mightily.

She also learned to appreciate her husband in ways she had previously taken for granted, and she learned to ask for help.

I realized that my marriage had been taken away from me for a higher cause—for God and country. I was sacrificing my marriage for the benefit of millions."

Not many families in the twenty-first century are challenged in the ways military families are.

My husband has been home for more than a year now, and we are officially back to normal. I made a promise to myself that I would never forget our year apart and have prayed that God would renew that feeling periodically so that I don't forget and fall prey to complacency.

Dangerous deployments are only one of the many challenges military wives have to face. There is a lot of loneliness. Additionally, training while at home is all consuming.

He leaves for work before 6:00 A.M. and he's usually not home until after 7:00 P.M.; that is, if he comes home at all. He spends many nights in the field training. In addition to knowing I will soon have to say good-bye to him again for an entire year, the little time I do have until he leaves is being taken up by training deployments. This summer he has two monthlong training deployments to other US bases. During those training exercises, I will not see him for those entire months. He is not permitted to have a cell phone, so his calls from pay phones are sporadic and often come at very inconvenient times. There are also the frustrating missed calls that come when I either can't get to the phone in time or the sound of the ring goes unnoticed in a noisy room. Hearing those messages are heartbreaking because I know it may be days until I get to speak to him again.

—married one year

Even time at home can be filled with pressure as deployment looms constantly.

Besides missing him when he is gone, the constant absences also make it difficult when he is home. Because our time together is so limited, there is a lot of pressure to make the most out of that time. I feel a need to spend every spare minute with him as though I were stocking up time before he deploys for a year. I have not gotten a job for that very reason. Although he spends a lot of time away training, the army tries to make up for it by giving him a lot of four-day weekends and long block leaves. If I were working at a regular civilian job, I would be at work when he has time off, and I was not willing to sacrifice that time with him. I am glad I made the decision not to work, and I am grateful that I do have the time to be with him. However, when he is gone for weeks at a time, I am left with nothing to do.

A wife of one year to a marine officer trained herself over a yearlong engagement period to give up her own expectations. "My father always told me that expectations are resentments under construction." When she finally learned to put everything in God's hands and just run with whatever came her way, she was and still is so much happier. Traveling together to new bases, meeting new people, and living in many different parts of the country has been exciting as she embraces life as a US Marine Corps wife, a life full of surprises. "I can't wait to see what God has in store for our future!"

> Despite the fear, loneliness, uncertainty, and frustration, I continue to be overwhelmed with how proud I am of my husband. There have been horrible days. I can't describe the irritation I felt when I learned he would be gone an extra month for training, or how frightened I was when he told me the plans had changed and he would not be going to Afghanistan, but instead to Iraq. I have never been more enraged than the day I learned he would not be getting out of the army this winter, as we had planned, but rather that he would be deployed again and serve an extra year and a half. It is instances like these that leave me feeling angry and resentful. However, time and time again, these emotions are surpassed by the rewards that come from understanding the importance of his work.
>
> —married one year

Many hardships have been endured and carried with grace for all the years of the life of our country. Perhaps their heart cry has been much the same as this wife of one year:

> I am so proud of my husband's decision to join the military, but the truth is, on my own, I almost certainly would not have made such an admirable and respectable decision. I am probably too selfish to have been willing to put my life on hold to serve my country. Therefore, I am overwhelmed with gratitude toward my husband for allowing me to be a participant in the honorable choice he made. I know I am not the one who goes overseas and fights, but every sacrifice I have made to be supportive of his efforts serves the same purpose.

fourteen

Children?

"Sons are a heritage from the Lord, children a reward from him."
—Psalm 127:3

The wedding is over. Rose petals have been thrown. The honeymoon has come and gone. Married life is settling in. Two questions begin to emerge: "When do you want to start having children?" and "How many children do you want to have?"

Having children. It is important to communicate about this subject.

A wife of six years emphasizes the importance of knowing how your husband feels about children. Some questions to ask might be: "Does he enjoy playing with children and taking care of them?" and "How does he feel about stay-at-home mothers?"

> I have had lots of friends with whom this has been an issue: the husband doesn't really like playing at length with their two-year-old, or bathing the six-month-old. He likes the *idea* of them, and that they will be grown up in the long run and more fun then; but as babies, he offers little help or support. Or the mother deeply desires to stay at home, and the husband is not willing to sacrifice the worldly things required to do so. Those are strong issues that can tear a marriage apart, and they are not issues we, as newly engaged (or even dating) couples think about to bring up. We assume if both of us want children, then we are on the same page. Not so. Children become your absolute world, and if you don't see the same way on the major issues, everything becomes a fight.

The first years of marriage are romantic, crazy, tough, exciting, stressful, and a continuous learning experience. Often, married couples start out thinking they have everything already decided and nothing will interrupt paradise. However, they quickly learn where they must make decisions and where compromise must happen. Communication—learning to tune out all other activities—is so important. This takes time.

> My husband and I just had our first child after three years of marriage. I am so thankful for the few years

we had to cultivate our marriage before starting a family. We decided when we got married that we wanted to take advantage of the freedom we had at that phase in life. We went on as many trips as we could afford, went to movies all the time, and went out to eat a lot. We built so many fun memories and had time to get to really know each other inside and out. Having a family now is such a blessing, but we wouldn't trade anything for the "us" time we had at the beginning of our marriage. I tell all my friends to not rush into having children, but to just enjoy each other for a while.

What a great plan, and it worked well for this couple. But plans can often be thwarted, calling for flexibility.

My husband and I were married for about six months when I started having trouble with the pill. My doctor changed me around to some different kinds, and before I knew it I was telling my newly-wed husband that we were pregnant. We really had a hard time soaking in the news. We were still getting comfortable with one another without my expanding waistline. I worried for so long that this new change would tear us apart. Now almost three years later, it is so obvious to me how richly blessed we are and how God has drawn us and our little girl closer together and closer to Him.

It is never too early to begin praying for the children you will have one day. Wisdom in parenting comes from above. Also, the timing when a child will be born is in God's hands.

What if there is no pregnancy?

> Once we decided to start trying to get pregnant, we prayed every night that God would bless us with a child and that it would happen according to His perfect timing. I then realized that that is what it is all about, His perfect timing. I continued to keep faith and hope that we would get pregnant and I still have that positive attitude today.

This wife of two years shares her story. After she sought medical advice, it was discovered that her progesterone level was extremely low, causing the need for a fertility drug. This drug was not without side effects—weight gain, moodiness, and cravings. The young woman felt so challenged in trying to get pregnant while at the same time explaining to her husband that she just didn't feel like herself.

> Husbands do not know exactly what we women go through, and I had to realize that mine never will. Don't get me wrong, I have a loving, caring, and understanding husband, but he couldn't understand my moods. At that time I realized fertility is nothing to be ashamed of, and I needed support and someone who could understand what I was facing. I contacted my closest friends and decided to email them as a group to keep them updated about my

doctor appointments and struggles with meds. And I could not have made it through without them. I also have a very close friend who has been going through fertility treatment for two years now. She was there for me and was someone who could say, "I understand, I have been there," and she always told me that she prayed for me and my husband daily. She helped me to realize that I wasn't going crazy as many days I felt I was, and that I didn't weigh 300 pounds, even though I felt like I did.

At this time a pregnancy has not occurred. Laparoscopic surgery has been performed to remove endometriosis. Artificial insemination was unsuccessful.

I continue to pray and keep hope. I know that things will happen in God's perfect timing and that gives me peace. I know that my friends are praying for me and supporting me. This is not something for anyone to have to go through alone. I also realize that it is OK that my husband may not fully understand.

The following poem was written after a good friend lost her baby to miscarriage.

Little baby sweet and dear,
Not tangible and yet so near,
Filled us with hopes, purposes, and dreams,
The light of so many . . . and yet it seems—
That our plans—once more—were not His best—
And again we are put to the test.

To believe His sovereignty
—His Absolute Rule,
He, our teacher
—Life, our school.
A little baby—a life yet to start,
Touched the depths of so many hearts.
Filled us with plans and preparations,
Anticipation and decorations.
We feel the loss—it's ours to bear,
And yet the child is with God and
      He deeply cares.

A sweet little baby—not to be born—
Will still impact this world so torn.
As people who observe those who gave it life
Are pointed to the one True Light.

Little baby up above—
May our loss be replaced
      With Christ's Love.

With love,
Donna Greene
July 1989

Although most entries in this book remain anonymous, the following story is meant to be shared with the world in its entirety.

Bradford and Stephen Phelan are a beautiful young 20-something couple. She went to Auburn University and is a teacher. He attended the University of Virginia undergraduate and law school as well. Stephen then graduated from Reformed Theological Seminary in Orlando, Florida, and is now a PCA minister in San Diego, California. They love and are committed to Jesus Christ.

I include this information because this couple is the picture of success in every way—intelligent, athletic, beautiful, purpose driven. Their entire lives have been filled with a continuous flow of excellence.

And yet, God has allowed them to experience pain on the deepest level. Listen to Bradford share her heart.

My Pregnancy Journey

"Naked I came from my mother's womb, and naked I will depart. The LORD gave and the LORD has taken away; may the name of the LORD be praised."

—Job 1:21

On December 29, 2003, Stephen and I found out that we were pregnant! The Lord gave. On January 23, 2004, Buddy Grace Phelan went to be with her Maker in heaven. The Lord had taken away.

On June 19, 2004, Stephen and I found out that we were pregnant. We had much more reservation, due to our first miscarriage. The Lord gave. On July 23, 2004, Mary Ella Phelan went to be with her Maker in heaven. The Lord had taken away.

May the name of the Lord be praised!

It has been two years since we began trying to have a baby, and we still do not have one to hold in our arms. However, we have two children who are in their perfect bodies in perfect peace with their

Jesus, and we can now begin to see that God has been transforming what has been bad and painful (miscarriages) into something glorious and good. It has taken me almost these full two years to get to the point where I can say that I do see my loving Father working in all of this for His glory and our good, as our pastor likes to say. The day we found out our child did not have a heartbeat, a lady said, "God works all thing together for the good." That is actually the last thing we wanted to hear at that moment. We knew that was truth deep down in our hearts, but in that moment of pain all we needed to hear was, "I am so sorry." We didn't need someone spouting off clichés and trying to give us answers. We just wanted to know that those who love us cared about us in our pain. It actually hurt most when people ignored that we were suffering and were too uncomfortable to even acknowledge that we were going through a hard time. Through the ups and downs and deep longings and screaming out to God, I have come to know my Father more deeply and do see His tender hand graciously molding our situation into good. Let me now explain some of my journey of going from *why* during our pregnancy trials to Who in hopes that it may bring you some healing and comfort as well.

On the morning of our eight-week appointment for our first pregnancy, I woke up early and began journaling. I wrote, "Dear Lord, I am so excited that I can hardly stand it! You are miraculous. You've brought an egg and sperm together and now, through Your power that is at work within me, our/Your child is forming and growing and developing into an image of You! Glory! Oh, I surrender this child to You for Your glory and purposes! Hallelujah! And, I trust it is in Your care. I do pray and long for it to be healthy and strong for Your glory! But I know Your will will be done. If it has any sort of defect, help us to receive the news with Your grace and mercy. Oh, we pray not. Thank You a billion times for this creation. You are our powerful Creator and Masterful Maker. Glory be to You!"

I did not even know what kind of pain I was on the brink of at that moment. I have always dreamed of being a mom. Since I can remember, I have said that I want to grow up and be a mom. And now, the excitement and anticipation of dreaming of being a mommy for years had piled up, and I felt like I might explode. Well, I almost did explode that day, but from sadness and not from joy. The doctor found no heartbeat. The tears freely came and I wept with my precious husband. I am even getting a bit choked up now, almost two years later, as I think about that moment of painful surprise. I remember saying, "Grace, her name is Grace." We had been referring to our child as Buddy, but when we later found out that our child had been a girl, we added Grace and now call her Buddy Grace. I highly suggest naming your miscarried child, no matter how early you miscarry, because it makes your child more real and alive in your heart. Well, God surely did give Stephen and me the grace to go through the next few days of suffering. He always shows up in a powerful way of grace in our greatest times of need. He is faithful. God used Psalm 23 to comfort me the afternoon after we received our bad news. He is my Shepherd and I knew He would shepherd me through this "valley of the shadow of death." The word "shadow" really comforted me. Our little child's death was only a mere shadow. Jesus took the actual death we all deserved so that we might one day "'dwell in the house of the Lord forever." What great news of the gospel.

The Lord gave me many divine appointments throughout our miscarriages to guide me when I was having a crisis of faith. Soon after our first loss, God brought the mother of one of my new friends into my path. I had never met this wonderful lady. She happened to be visiting from Hawaii the week after my miscarriage. My friend called me and said that her mom, who is a counselor and who had four miscarriages herself, would love to talk with me to encourage and love on me. Well, the Lord did use her profoundly to bring me hope and new perspective. Her empathetic counsel was to focus on God's character. She reminded me that God's character never changes and that it is always good, just, and caring. She said, "You'll never get to heaven and say, 'Lord, this and this weren't fair.'" She instructed me to say, "Lord, Your character is what I'm choosing to focus on, not my circum- stances." This is when my focus began to shift from the question of why to who. Miscarriages were not in God's perfect original plan; however, He is the loving "who" in the middle of the trial, over the pain, and under my weak frame. In my suffering, I found the loving, gentle hand of my heavenly Daddy, and He held me.

Another divine appointment the Lord gave us after our second miscarriage was when our pastor and his wife came over to our home and cried with us and counseled us. Our pastor, Dick, reminded us that "the kingdom has come, but it has not yet come in full" (see Matthew 6:10). Jesus left His Spirit with us, so the kingdom is here, but not in full. So we still have suffering while on this earth. But we can pray in confidence that the kingdom will come because we know Jesus is coming back to make all things right and new! That helped me in my confusion and sadness. I was also confused about how to pray. I tried to pray in faith after our first miscarriage that we would have no more early terminated pregnancies. Stephen and I even went to a healing service. Yet, here we were again, mourning the death of our child. Dick encouraged us to pray with all our hearts for healthy pregnancies. Yet, if we have another unhealthy pregnancy that ends in miscarriage, it requires even more faith to believe God's good plan even when we don't understand. And again, we must remember that the kingdom's not here yet in full. We act as if we are God if we think that it all depends on how much faith we have and how little doubt we have. We must not focus on the quantity of our faith but the quality. Focus on who our faith is in—Jesus

Christ! God proved that He does transform all things into good through the cross. The cross was the most evil event of all history, and God transformed it into the most glorious event in all history. This does not mean that a miscarriage is good, just as the cross was not good. But all things are transformed into good purposes. Dick also used the story of Lazarus's death to comfort us in our mourning. In John 11:33, the Word says that Jesus was "deeply moved in spirit and troubled." The Greek translation of this verse is that Jesus was "snorting with anger." Our pastor soothed us with the truth that Jesus was snorting with anger and weeping with us, just as He wept with Lazarus's sisters, even when He knew that Lazarus would be raised from the dead. We can be sad and mad at death because Jesus was. What relief and comfort.

After almost two years since we began trying to get pregnant, God is showing us one tangible good that He is working in our situation: adoption. We are so excited about adopting that we can hardly stand it. I was actually bitter when people told us after our miscarriages, "Oh, at least you can adopt." That is not what grieving parents need to hear right after a miscarriage. But God prepared us for moving into adoption through many months of healing and crying out in anguish. The Lord particularly used a dream to put the call to adopt on my heart. The morning after the dream, I could hardly wait to call the Bethany Christian Services. We have been accepted in the initial procedures of this process and are now praying for the Lord to handpick our child for us. There is a new, different joy that is swelling up in our hearts as we anticipate receiving the blessings of a little infant whom God has chosen to bless us with. We still are hoping to get pregnant and to have a child naturally; but no matter what, we can say with all of our hearts, "God is good, and His ways are higher than ours. Blessed be the name of the Lord!"

Bible verses that God used to heal me:

Psalm 84:10: "Better is one day in your courts than a thousand elsewhere."

Psalm 116:15: "Precious in the sight of the LORD is the death of his saints."

Psalm 22:9–10, 31: "Yet you brought me out of the womb; you made me trust in you even at my mother's breast. From birth I was cast upon you; from my mother's womb you have been my God. . . . They will proclaim his righteousness to a people yet unborn."

Psalm 71:1, 3, 5: "In You, O LORD, I have taken refuge. . . . Be my rock of refuge, to which I can always go; give the command to save me, for you are my rock and my fortress. . . . For you have been my hope, O Sovereign LORD, my confidence since my youth. From birth I have relied on you. You brought me forth from my mother's womb. I will ever praise you."

Psalm 16:1–2, 5–6, 8–9, 11: "Keep me safe, O God, for in you I take refuge. I said to the LORD, 'You are my Lord; apart from you I have no good thing.' . . . LORD, you have assigned me my portion and my cup; you have made my lot secure. The boundary lines have fallen for me in pleasant places; surely I have a delightful inheritance. . . . I have set the LORD always before me. Because he is at my right hand, I will not be shaken. Therefore my heart is glad and my tongue rejoices; my body will also rest secure. . . . You have made known to me the path of life; you will fill me with joy in your presence, with eternal pleasures at your right hand."

Ecclesiastes 3:1–2: "There is a time . . . and a season for every activity under heaven: a time to be born and a time to die."

Psalm 113, especially verse 9: "He settles the barren woman in her home as a happy mother of children. Praise the LORD."

Philippians 3:7–9: "Whatever was to my profit, I now consider loss for the sake of Christ. What is more, I consider everything a loss compared to the surpassing greatness of knowing Christ Jesus my Lord, for whose sake I have lost all things. I consider them rubbish, that I may gain Christ and be found in him, not having a righteousness of my own . . ., but that which is through faith in Christ."

Books/CDs that were helpful during my miscarriages:

CD:

Watermark, *All Things New*, track 6: "Glory Baby" (Rocketown Records)

Books:

Grieving the Child I Never Knew: A Devotional Companion for Comfort in the Loss of Your Unborn or Newly Born Child, by Kathe Wunnenberg (Zondervan, 2001)

Empty Arms: Hope and Support for Those Who Have Suffered a Miscarriage, Stillbirth, or Tubal Pregnancy, by Pam Vredevelot (Multnomah, 2001)

Free to Grieve, by Maureen Rank (Bethany House, 2004)

Like many couples, when my husband and I were first married, we made plans and goals for our life together, including where we would live, what jobs we would have, and when we would begin having children. We were confident of our plans and hoped that they would be God's plan for our lives as well. God did allow many of the things we wanted to come to pass; and when I became pregnant a few months after we started trying to conceive, we thought our dream of having children was coming true as well. But God had a different path for us to take.

This young couple also saw their dreams shattered as two pregnancies ended in miscarriage. The first baby's death marked the beginning of a long and painful struggle with infertility.

My husband and I were heartbroken after our loss and continued trying to have a baby, only to conceive again and miscarry. The doctors didn't know why this was happening. One specialist even said it was just "bad luck." We knew God was allowing this struggle for a reason, but we didn't know why. All of our other friends seemed to be having children so easily. We received many birth announcements and invitations to our friends' baby showers, and we were truly happy for them. But why was God not allowing us to be parents too? We cried out to the Lord, but we remained childless.

Months of trying turned into years as we waited. They were the most difficult years of my life. My incredible husband loved me and encouraged me when I was down, and through these tough years our marriage grew stronger. But I couldn't understand how he could go to work each day and forget about our struggles. Having a baby had become an idol in my life.

Finally, after a few years of miscarriages, tests, blood work, fertility drugs, and the ups and downs that come with thinking this might be "the month," we received a call from a nurse at our doctor's office. She said we were expecting a baby, but that my hormone levels were so low that if it were possible, she would say we were "sort of pregnant." I was so excited, yet so scared at the same time.

This young woman recalls going into her bedroom and literally falling down on the floor with her arms open as she cried out to God.

> This was His baby and if He wanted to take it home, then please do it soon. But if He wanted us to have it, then that's what we wanted. I asked Him to please save the baby, but that we wanted His plan, not ours. After I said that, I felt a peace I hadn't felt before. Of course, the baby was in His hands all along, but I had to be willing to let go of my desires and trust Him completely. I did not know what would happen, but I knew it was in our loving Father's hands. I would have to trust His plan.

Nine months later she gave birth to a beautiful baby boy.

> Words can't describe the joy and thankfulness my husband and I felt at that moment and still to this day. As I write this now many years later, all of the emotions I felt during the infertility process are coming back to me as brief reminders of the pain and longing we experienced. I know God used that time of waiting to grow our relationship with Him and with each other. I think of Proverbs 19:21 which says, "Many are the plans in a man's heart, but it is the Lord's purpose that prevails." He still loves all of us and His plan is best.

Following are listed a few things that helped her during that struggle or that she wished she had been better at doing.

1. *Pray* for wisdom (and patience) regarding your choice of doctors, procedures, and fertility options that are available.
2. Gather information and talk about these options with your husband. Agree on the course of action you want to take. For instance, do you want to take fertility drugs or not? Are you open to adoption should the Lord lead you there? There are many options out there, so pray about them with your spouse.
3. Talk with a person you trust or admire who has struggled with fertility. When I had my first miscarriage, I thought other people wouldn't understand what I was going through. But once I talked about it, I discovered many people who had experienced miscarriages too. It helped me to know there were other women who would understand.
4. Don't let trying to have a child consume you, as it did me for a while. It can distract you from your relationship with God and your husband. God wants us to love Him most.
5. Enjoy the time you have right now with your husband . . . just the two of you. Do fun things together as much as possible.

For those who do not struggle with infertility and wish to help a friend who experiences this.

1. Ask your friend how she is doing. You'll get a sense of whether or not she wants to talk about it. (It helped me to talk about my struggle and to know that my friends cared enough to ask. Of course, there were days I just didn't want to talk so I just said so.)
2. Pray for your friend, and perhaps call or write her a note to let her know you're doing so.
3. Don't give advice such as, "Just relax. It'll happen soon if you do." I can't tell you how many times I heard things like that. I know the person meant it as encouragement, but it wasn't the kind of thing I wanted to hear.
4. If you're with a group of moms, don't let the conversation focus only on children. Be sensitive to your friend's feelings and find some other topics that she can talk about too.
5. If you know someone else who has experienced infertility, ask your friends if they would like to meet or talk with each other.

—married seven years

The Lord does have a plan and a purpose for each one of His children. Just as there are no two people alike, there are no two plans alike. God's ways are perfect and His plans also.

My eyes brimmed with tears as I considered the new meaning of the old familiar words. I was back in church after a seven-week journey in Ukraine where my husband and I had just adopted our first child. I had always appreciated the beauty of the great hymn "Praise to the Lord, the Almighty," but today it was deeply and powerfully personal as my voice and heart cried out, "Hast thou not seen how thy desires e'er have been granted in what He ordaineth?"

My husband and I had longed for a child, and as we had prayed and waited and waited and prayed, we wondered how God would fulfill this longing. We began to consider the beauty of adoption and sensed that somewhere in the world there could be a child planned by our heavenly Father to be a part of our family. The journey was not easy and there were many stressful, anxious moments as we traveled this path. Yet those anxieties faded when we met our precious son. We were amazed at how quickly our hearts overflowed with love for him, and it is now abundantly clear that God had unfolded His perfect plan in our lives.

Yes, I have truly seen how my desires have been granted in what He has ordained.

—married four years

 *fifteen*

Leaving and Cleaving

"Don't urge me to leave you or to turn back from you. Where you go I will go, and where you stay I will stay. Your people will be my people and your God my God."

—Ruth 1:16

The minister concludes the marriage ceremony: "I now pronounce you husband and wife." In a matter of minutes, a man and a woman are not only no longer single—they have now become a new family. The Bible clearly states that in a marriage there is leaving and cleaving. But what does this involve? How do you sort out your relationship with your family, his family? Where do you live? What is normal?

"And they lived happily ever after." What a myth! And especially in marriage. The difficulties in marriage are plagued by a tremendous assortment of misconceptions about what marriage should be. What we anticipate seldom occurs, and what we least expect generally happens. Everyone lives by a set of unspoken rules and tends to play roles, unconscious though they may be. Every person enters into marriage with his or her own set of commandments about what is normal. Most of us assume that our rules of normal are universal, and they almost always come from families of origin. There is no single force that comes close to the power of the family when it comes to imprinting our unspoken sense of normal.

Questions you might have:
1. What does a normal husband look like?
2. What does a normal wife look like?
3. What does a normal marriage look like?
4. What is a normal way to deal with conflict?
5. What about holidays?

The list goes on and on, but important to remember is that unless there is clear communication, there will be conflict. Rules will be broken that the spouse never knew existed and some discovered that had never been put into words. Frustration and misunderstanding are certainties as each spouse becomes irritated by the other's unspoken expectations and angered because the other did not live by the same rules.

The expectations of what a marriage should be can make or break it. Don't assume the myth that "we think alike." The more openly differing expectations are discussed, the more likely a vision of what your marriage should look like will occur. Seek to be honest about issues brought into marriage. Pretending differences don't exist leads to disaster.

> It is funny that whenever we are having a misunderstanding, argument, sometimes we just start laughing because we realize that we may have different opinions but it is not like we are going to give up or call it quits. It is not worth it to continue going on and on about whatever we are discussing. We say, "We will agree to disagree."
>
> —married three years

Beginning as a new family means you now become part of your spouse's family also—one that has different expectations, traditions, and values from your own. Relationship with in-laws is crucial. At times it may feel completely normal, but at other times it may be overwhelming.

> The most important thing that my mom told me about marriage was that when my mother-in-law/ father-in-law are getting on my nerves to remember that if it were not for them that I would not have my husband. I have had to remind myself of that so many times. We have a difficult time with my in-laws around the holidays. It is hard to make everyone happy. Luckily, my parents have always said that they will not ever make us feel guilty about our holiday plans—that helps out so much!
>
> —married three years

How important to avoid mentioning any fights or disagreements you are having with your spouse when you're with your in-laws or your own family.

A wife should always remember to never speak negatively about your husband to anyone, especially your own family (mainly your mom!) because you may forget the little problems that you are venting about, but your momma will most likely never forget them and will (whether or not she means to) hold them against your husband. Hit your knees when you feel the urge to complain or compare notes with others. Ask God to show you your *own* sin and humble you, that you can rightly respond to your husband.

—married four years

Leaving and cleaving may take many forms. A wife of six years was married six months after college graduation. Although she loved her hometown, she had always wanted to move away after marriage. Her husband, however, was offered a wonderful job and felt that it was God's plan for them to stay.

While I loved my hometown, I was sad and frustrated because I had dreamed of us starting our adventure in a different town. I knew that I had to make the most of it. I was worried that by living here, I wouldn't learn how to rely on my husband.

Living that close to my parents I felt would tempt me to run to them whenever I was sad, hurt, or needed money (ha, ha) instead of my husband. Through prayer, God protected me from that and allowed my husband to be my family. He taught me how to truly "leave and cleave," but at the same time have an incredible relationship with my parents. They will always be my parents and nothing could take away the love I feel for them.

She felt that her marriage was blessed by their seeking the Lord together.

Another young wife of two years shares her story. God's plan for her marriage included moving completely across the United States.

Three months after my husband and I married, God opened an opportunity for us in the Pacific Northwest. With God's will and the lure of adventure tugging at our hearts, we moved 2,000 miles to the west. That was two years ago.

These first two years of marriage have certainly met our expectations for adventure. We have explored beautiful facets of the West together and have met many new people. Despite these pockets of adventure, it has been difficult for me to be so far from family, friends, and the culture in which I was raised. My husband and I live in a unique area of the country that has its own indigenous religion and lifestyle. There are times when I am lonely and homesick, uncertain of my place in these new environs. These are the times when I have clung to my husband for support, for affirmation, security, love, friendship; the list could go on and on. The poor man! God has given me my ideal helpmate, the man with whom I share my life's purpose. He is a faithful and loving husband, the husband I have always prayed for, but he is only human!

This experience has taught her not only to cleave to her husband but also to lean on the Lord for her true support.

I think it is a common trap to rely on your husband to meet all of your needs, whether they are emotional, spiritual, or physical. Our society advocates the "you complete me" image of marriage in which a husband's and wife's expectations for each other are so high and ultimately cannot be fulfilled. God has challenged me in these last years and has gently pushed me to realize that although I live in this very different place so far from home, I cannot expect my husband (wonderful though he is) to meet my every need for lover, friend, protector, guardian, companion, etc. Those are all names for Christ, and while a husband *certainly* has a role in fulfilling pieces of those characteristics, only God can fill in *all* the holes. Marriage is a relationship with your husband, but much more importantly, it is a relationship between you, your husband, and your glorious heavenly Father.

Whether you live in the town where you grew up or halfway around the world, know that there will be times when you feel down and out. Rather than looking to your right to desperately cling to your husband's arm, just hold his hand in yours and look to God. That is a blessed picture of marriage, and what a beautiful union it is!

A change of plans caused another couple to actually move in with her parents for longer than expected.

My husband and I have been living with my parents for 9 of our first 24 months of marriage, something neither of us anticipated. When my husband's job in New York fell through at the last minute, we found ourselves moving back home. At first, living with my parents felt like a long vacation since we thought we'd be living with them for only a few weeks—2 months at most—until we found jobs. When we became employed and bought a house, our jobs kept us so busy that we barely had the time to focus on fixing it up. Somehow, 9 months have passed and we're still here. I would never recommend living with your parents as long as we have. In retrospect, if we had known it would take this long, we probably would have rented an apartment.

Marriage has changed for this couple.

Living with my parents has temporarily changed our marriage dynamic, and according to Mom, that's a two-way street. Communication and romance can be lacking at times. I'd say our sex life isn't exactly spontaneous with my parents always around. There is no private place to discuss issues, which makes us more likely to fight because of the lack of communication. In fact, we've actually had big fights *about* living with my parents *in front of* my parents. There was nowhere else to go! Before we moved in with my parents, we never realized how much time previously spent cleaning, cooking, washing dishes, and doing routine chores was actually time spent hanging out and communicating with each other. Now, my parents are around 100 percent of the time. The only time we have with each other is when everyone goes to bed, and by then we are usually so tired that we fall asleep once our heads hit the pillow.

With a moving date in sight, she reflects:

My husband and I are very fortunate that my parents are probably the kindest, most understanding, and most laid-back parents ever. Mom fixes dinner, packs our lunches, picks up our dry cleaning, and keeps the house clean. We certainly don't deserve to be so spoiled. We couldn't be more thankful for her help, especially when we're both working very long hours. Also, since we're not paying utility bills or buying food, we have saved tons of money. We've been able to afford improvements to our house that previously were not in our budget. Also, we haven't had to live in the mess of construction.

It's hard not to get frustrated at my parents when I feel like they're invading the few moments of privacy I have with my husband. I have to remember it's we who are invading their space, and they're selflessly letting us do so without complaining. However, despite the frustration, there has been an upside to all this. Life is short and incredibly hectic. There never seems to be enough time spent with loved ones, and any quality time we have with them is a gift to be appreciated. Though we have to make a concerted effort to keep communication lines open and we have to physically leave home for any privacy, in the end I feel like the time will be cherished.

Move-in day is next week, and my husband and I are going to have a whole new appreciation for time alone with each other, and for our own parents as well.

Leaving and cleaving takes time. Matrimony is a process that matures slowly. In biblical times, the special status of bride and groom lasted a full year.

"If a man has recently married, he must not be sent to war or have any other duty laid on him. For one year he is to be free to stay at home and bring happiness to the wife he has married."
—Deuteronomy 24:5

I've heard it put, "Marriage is not about your happiness but your holiness." I think that is wisdom. Marriage isn't easy. It's a commitment, and commitment takes work. As you both work together, you're sanctified in Christ. Only Christ is the perfect Bridegroom. So, look to Jesus. Don't expect too much of your spouse or yourself. But if anything, point the finger inward at yourself and see ways you could be loving your spouse better. If you are constantly critical of your spouse and focus on the shortcomings, your love is snuffed out a bit. As you seek to serve and love your spouse better, your spouse in turn begins to love and serve you more. It is amazing. So look to Jesus, the perfect lover, to give you love. And look to Jesus, the One who denied Himself into death, to enable you to deny yourself and put your spouse's needs above your own.

—married three years

sixteen

"For Better or for Worse"

"Love is patient, love is kind. It does not envy, it does not boast, it is not proud. It is not rude, it is not self-seeking, it is not easily angered, it keeps no record of wrongs. Love does not delight in evil but rejoices with the truth. It always protects, always trusts, always hopes, always perseveres. Love never fails."

—1 Corinthians 13:4–8

It is not unusual for many couples to float through their first years of marriage in a blissful state. But, for others, the early years of marriage may be a very difficult adjustment. Marriage is a prime place for God to develop His love and attributes into the hearts of two very imperfect human beings. The rough edges of sinful nature are chipped and filed off as each partner bumps against one another.

"As iron sharpens iron, so one man sharpens another."
—Proverbs 27:17

A beautiful young woman, a decorator, shares her insights in preparing for the physical aspects of a new home.

> You don't have to wait to get married before buying furniture. I have been collecting since graduating from college! I have found that if you buy classic and versatile pieces—not temporary ones—you'll have them forever! Remember you are not just furnishing for your first house but buying for your second one as well. I had furniture stored at my parents' and grandmother's houses for years before I could finally use it. One of my favorite rules of thumb is, if you buy right the first time, you'll only cry once.

Marriage is meant for a lifetime, but just as this woman began planning for her actual home many years before the wedding day, the building blocks that stand strong are laid with care over a period of many years to establish a marriage that will last in good times and in bad. The reality of a lifetime commitment can be overwhelming, as is shared by this bride of less than a year.

> I will begin with the engagement period because that is when I first recognized the changes in my life. More than the fear that people sometimes

describe, of being committed to someone for the rest of your life, I felt that responsibility and the anxiety of being part of this two-person team that I had just signed myself up for! I began to worry more and more each day about things like one of us getting a life-threatening disease or being hurt or killed in a car accident—or not even making it to the wedding day. It was awful. The engagement time is hard because you are counting on everything leading up to this one day and you are just hoping that you both make it to the day. (This is why I always recommend a short engagement!)

Finally, I had come to the point where I forced myself to sit down with the Lord and ask Him to carry these burdensome thoughts and ideas that were swimming in my head. I wanted so much to enjoy the engagement time, and I definitely did after I chose to let God control my thoughts rather than this sinful world. I was afraid that if He took my husband from me, I wouldn't be able to handle it—but I know that the Lord wants the best for His children and that He would never give me something that I couldn't handle with Him by my side. So, after reminding myself of these key points of a joyful life, I was able to put aside my anxiety and let the joy of Christ fill me before the wedding—and now it has spilled over into our marriage!

All marriages will have bumps in the road. Life is filled with ups and downs. There are good days as well as bad ones and as human beings, we have little control over many of the situations in life and often have little warning concerning those hard and difficult times.

Such difficulties are as follows:

Health

God has a way of showing you things he wants you to learn about yourself and about those that you love. Graham and I had been dating six months when the doctors told me I had cancer for the second time. By the look on his face and the fear in his eyes, I knew how much I really meant to him. After three surgeries, a monthlong hospital stay, and seven weeks of radiation, I knew he was the one. I think I would have known this without having to go through all of that, but God has His way of showing you exactly what you need. Graham never left my side. Spending the night in hospitals was not something a normal 20-year-old guy did, but Graham did it with a smile on his face. He was my rock and my angel sent straight from God. We both hoped and prayed that this would be the last time we ever had to go through this, but unfortunately we experienced a lighter version two years later. Once again, Graham was there! I was so sorry he had to experience so much fear and frustration at such a young age, but he never blinked an eye. Six months later, I was due for another MRI to see if the cancer had returned. I got a clean bill of health and Graham proposed that night. I don't know if he realized, but I know it was God's way of saying, "You are finished. Have all the joy and glory this man can offer." Graham proved himself "through sickness and health" before we said our vows. God showed me the loving man He created before we were married and I am so thankful!

—Neillie Kirk Tayloe

Husband in Substance Abuse

"And the two shall become one flesh." How true that does feel as you marry and begin a life together. Two separate, distinct lives becoming one in the Lord. What affects one has a profound effect on the other. Whether in joy or in pain, one takes on celebration or suffering of the other.

Being that we had become one in the Lord, I knew for quite a while something wasn't quite right with my husband and in our marriage. I would frequently talk to the Lord and ask for wisdom and insight. Things weren't terrible, but I knew it was not the marriage the Lord had designed it to be. One peaceful summer day, talking to the Lord while sitting on our screened-in porch, I wrote in my journal the following: "Lord, if there is something that I need to know, would You bring it to light, and would You do it quickly?" For whatever reason, on that day there was such heaviness in my heart and burden for our marriage that was about more than I could take. Well, God was faithful to hear and answer my prayer, as eight days later He brought not just a light, but a high beam.

In a way that only God could have orchestrated, I learned that my husband (whom I had been married to quite a few years) had been using marijuana and not just occasionally, but daily, and not just for a short while, but for many years. *So what?* many might say, *that's no big deal of a drug.* To me, it was a big deal. It was a huge deal. That drug had robbed my husband of much and had begun to rob me and our children as well. Here I was, having asked the Lord to reveal to me anything that needed to be brought to light, yet I was angry that I needed to deal with something like this in my life.

Having the opportunity of now being able to look back on those hard times, I see how much the Lord used that event in my husband's life as a tool of great growth in my own life. I had no idea over the course of months that the Lord would dig so deep inside of me to clean out all of the "yuck" I had—it was my husband who was the one with the problem! What He did reveal to me was "for *all* have sinned, and fall short of the glory of God" (Romans 3:23). In my anger I wanted to point the finger at my husband, who outwardly was sinning, but the Lord turned my own finger back on myself and seemingly said, "Take the log out of your own eye before you try to take the speck out of another; you are full of pride" (see Matthew 7:3–5). I thought I had it all figured out. I was walking with the Lord, doing all that I thought He would intend for me to do, yet the Lord showed me that my spiritual pride has swelled so large I was the one who needed the change.

Well, we both have changed. My husband has more than I have. There is still so much work to be done in that area of my life. In the beginning for my husband, as he put it so well, not doing the drug has been for him "like learning to write left-handed when you have been right-handed for so long." He had to learn to respond to everything in such a different way than he had for so long. There was no more escaping. It took time; it seemed like a long time. There were bumps along the way. There were times I'm sure he wanted to go back to his old way of life, and there were times I just wanted to run away from it all. However, I can tell you God *is* faithful and He is "restoring the years that the locusts have eaten" (see Joel 2:25–27).

I've decided that God ordained marriage as a means of sanctification in a believer's life! I'm not sure how theologically correct that is, but it sure does feel it. God has used my husband to bring me into a deeper relationship with my Savior, which is so appropriate, as it was my husband who introduced me to Him to begin with.

—Anonymous

Adultery

Please tell your married girls to never give up, never ever give up! We serve a God of miracles who parted the Red Sea for His chosen people and He parted the Red Sea for my marriage. A few years into our marriage, my husband started having an affair with someone at work. I found out about five years later, when he told me himself! From past experience, I had learned that divorce is not the answer to your problems. Often your problems just become greater as a result. I was committed to my husband even though he was struggling with his commitment to me. Clearly the Holy Spirit kept bringing to my mind the children of Israel. God continuously worked miracles on their behalf and they repeatedly forgot His miracles. I did not want to forget the many miracles God had worked in my life. One passage I clung to was Exodus 14:13–14: "Moses answered the people, 'Do not be afraid. Stand firm and you will see the deliverance the Lord will bring you today. The Egyptians you see today you will never see again. The Lord will fight for you; you need only to be still.'"

Now, five years later, with lots of counseling and lots of long hours learning how to communicate, God has drastically changed both of us and He has blessed us with a healthy marriage. A marriage that is now built on a strong foundation to withstand the many outside storms that still come our way. I am so thankful that I did not listen to the conventional wisdom of the day that when things get tough, find someone else. If I could marry my husband over again, I would! God indeed is the God of miracles in my life!

—Anonymous

Katrina

On Friday as I was leaving school, I was extremely stressed about the fact that the majority of my students had done poorly on their math quizzes. In a matter of days, my stress was completely shifted; I was now worried about my house, the safety of friends, my return to New Orleans, and I soon realized that those quizzes would never be given back to the owners.

Hurricane Katrina was an eye-opening experience for many, including myself. It is amazing how one day you can be doing one thing, living one place, and the next day your life can be completely uprooted and what you know as your routine entirely lost. My focuses are no longer on the small stresses of everyday life, but are now moved to things that last and are important in the big picture. Remember the importance of family because you will never know when you may need to be sharing a house again. Always remind people that you love them through the bad times and good, as many have a tendency to forget the latter. And, finally, allow yourself to be adaptable because you never know when you will need to be.

—Jeanne Upchurch de'Laureal

The Disappearance of Natalee Holloway

When I describe how Rusty proposed to me, people halfway smile, a little confused. It seems very simple and unromantic. The middle of the afternoon? On my sofa in my living room? No ring? Nothing I ever pictured. Had God revealed in advance to me the circumstances of my proposal, I would have begged and pleaded for a different one. But it couldn't have been more perfect or more revealing about God's love for me and His love for our union. In fact, my proposal included everything I wanted. It was breathtaking. In a moment when I felt smothered by a million different emotions,

Rusty took my breath away and gave new life to my soul when he committed his life to me by asking me to be his wife. His words were like music and his own tears, my flowers. I experienced the best mountaintop high sitting right there on my sofa. I never knew the love of this man could lift me out of the pit I felt trapped in and dust me off and make me feel like a beautiful princess. My heart, I thought, was empty from days of sorrow and confusion. And now, in an instant, it was full. God's hand had ordained this specific moment in time. Rusty had become more than my fiancé, and I could see how he was indeed made for me, for this moment. His words were life-giving, not only to me, but to others.

You see, for the past three years (two of which Rusty and I were dating), I had been Natalee Holloway's discipleship leader. She and all her friends had been so important to me, and it was no secret to Rusty that they came first. In fact, Rusty had been teased about not proposing until they graduated so I could give them my all until they left for college. It was on that same sofa that week after week, Natalee and her friends had sat and listened to God's words and promises. It was in that room that we had joined hands and prayed. My sofa. My living room. And from where Rusty kneeled, he faced the outside deck, where just a month before I had celebrated with the girls their graduation in an elaborate dinner. June 4, just five days after Natalee disappeared, the man I loved most in this world was asking me to be his wife.

In the midst of the chaos, hurt, uncertainty of me and these precious friends of Natalee's, he was also asking for the responsibility of comforting me and filling me up—no matter what. Rusty knew how important these girls are to me, and my engagement was a much-needed smile for many of us.

Obviously, my engagement was not typical. But I think it was very realistic. Do I think Rusty planned to do it when tragedy struck? No, of course not. But I do think God used Rusty to show both of us our love for each other in very real ways. Marriage is very serious. God's timing for Rusty and me almost completely cast a shadow on the wedding and shines this bright glowing light on our marriage. I have no doubt how Rusty will provide for me emotionally and spiritually—I have seen it. And I would say Rusty has no doubt on how I will respond to his gifts of love and support—because in the wake of the chaos, I accepted them—as stubborn as I am, I accepted them gladly, almost helplessly. For the gift of that moment in time, I praise and thank God for the perfect proposal.

—Elizabeth Sandner Rich

Tsunami

Following J. T.'s graduation from law school, we decided to celebrate by backpacking through Nepal, India, Laos, Vietnam, Cambodia, and Thailand. The trip was an amazing opportunity for us to spend time with each other and experience different cultures together.

December 26, 2004, was to be our last day of a 12-week trip. We were on Phi Phi Island in southern Thailand. Phi Phi Island is a little strip of beach (packed with shops and bungalows) that connects two uninhabited mountains. There is a bay on each side of the beach. It was then that the Indian Ocean tsunami hit. It left us stranded on the island for two days and one night.

This had been our first Christmas away from home, and Christmas on the island was far from a celebration of Christ's birth. It felt so empty. J. T. wanted to hike to the top of the mountain to read his Bible and spend time with God. Up to that point, we hadn't left the beach for eight days. J. T. was reading First John, and I was enjoying the views. A few minutes later, we noticed the bay start receding almost like a bathtub being drained. At first we thought it was low tide, but it kept going and going until the sea floor and coral reefs were exposed. Then we saw the massive wall of water. We watched in disbelief as it picked up strength, crossed over the entire strip of beach, and washed almost everything out into the bay on the other side.

J. T. and I ran down the mountain to help in any way we could. When we got to the bottom, there was complete destruction as far as the eye could see. Even cement building foundations were destroyed. The spot on the beach where we had been just 15 minutes before was unrecognizable. It was eerily quiet, but every now and then we heard a cry for help.

We sat down and prayed together that God would guide every decision we would make in these critical moments. During the next few hours, J. T. and I witnessed the most gruesome sights we had ever seen. Sometimes I wondered if it would not be better to be dead than as badly maimed as some of these people were. J. T. helped pull bodies out of the debris while I comforted injured people. With nothing but bed sheets and beach towels to wrap up wounds, I've never felt so helpless in my life. It was several hours before the first chopper surveyed the island. Even when they started coming and going regularly, there just weren't enough.

Everyone who spent the night on the mountainside around us had lost loved ones. One woman approached me and asked if I had seen any of her four children. They had all washed away, and she couldn't find them. I vividly remember sitting there, looking out to what we could see of the debris in the darkness, and trying to comprehend just how painful that would be. What if it were my husband buried under that mess or severely injured and there was no way I could help? I wasn't able to process what was happening. It seemed like all of this would be over in a few days, and everyone would find their families and go back home. It was too painful to comprehend.

In some ways, what happened is harder to deal with now than when we were on the island, because the adrenaline has worn off. We often wonder *Why us?* and *How do we still have each other?* There is no reason we are alive, except for

God's mercy and grace. Our lives are completely out of our control and are in His hands. We did nothing to save ourselves. I realize that many Christians were probably washed away in the tsunami, and that if we were among them, God would still be the same God to me. As Christians, J. T. and I are so thankful to know that no matter what happens to us, our eternal hope is in something indestructible. Nothing can separate us from the love of God (Romans 8:38–39). It would be impossible to deal with such a situation without having a foundation more solid than life on earth. To be able to know, trust, and seek God despite being surrounded by misery was a tremendous comfort. It was our only comfort.

The memory of being amidst the destruction has not faded from our minds. We are so incredibly thankful for each day we have with each other. We give each other that many more hugs and that many more kisses. No moment is taken for granted. Even now, when I wake up at night and see J. T. next to me, I feel overwhelming relief and thankfulness. Seeing more than 2,000 healthy people killed in front of our eyes on just one tiny stretch of beach is a reminder of how fragile life is, and how your entire life can be changed in the blink of an eye. And it can happen when you least expect it.

—Caroline Dumas Malatesta

Husband in Medical Profession

While my husband and I were hiking, biking, etc., in God's beautiful Utah deserts, I prayed for

Him to please put on my heart what, if given the chance, to tell other young women married to men in the medical profession—especially surgery!

Immediately, I remembered what a very wise Christian mentor told me two years ago about marriage: picture a triangle with you and your spouse at the bottom two points of the triangle opposite each other, and picture God at the top point of the triangle. In marriage, if you are always focused on your relationship with God, your eyes and heart fixed on Him, then you are actually closer to your spouse. For example, if my utmost focus is my relationship with God and working to move closer to Him, then the distance between my spouse and me actually lessens *even if* my spouse is not in the same place spiritually.

The last point is very important for us women married to surgeons because I found myself diving deep into Bible studies and my Christian friends at a time when my husband was obligated to work crazy hours and always Sunday mornings and on the holidays when most people are in church—like Christmas and Easter. That being said, it is no surprise that at certain points in our relationship, I felt like we were on two totally different spiritual wavelengths when my husband could not see straight because he was so tired, yet I was beaming with a new love for God that I had witnessed at church that day. Many times that frustrated me, but when I went to prayer, God reminded me of that triangle.

Knowing that the absence of church and study was totally out of my husband's control during certain phases of a general surgery residency led me to prayer. My prayers for him were for Christian mentors at the hospital—doctors, nurses, patients, etc. Many times in the medical setting there are many men and women (especially surgeons) who think *they* may actually be God (!), so my constant prayer for my husband is a humble heart and Christian mentors, and also that God constantly show Himself to my husband as the Great Physician. And God has answered this prayer numerous times—sometimes in the most unexpected ways via the families of patients, etc.

Finally, there are two books that I highly recommend: *The Power of the Praying Wife* by Stormie Omartian (Harvest House Publishers, 2007) and *Devotions for Couples* by Patrick Morley (Zondervan, 1994).

—married three years

My husband and I married during his second year of medical school. I had heard about the difficulties of being married to a doctor, much less to one in training. However, it really did not hit me until we moved to Nashville for residency at Vanderbilt.

Growing up, I had always been an independent person. I preferred to have a lot of friends but one really close one. I seldom had a boyfriend who went to the same school as I did. Even in college, I went to an all-girls school and had a boyfriend at a nearby school whom I saw one night a week and on weekends. This, in a way, prepared me for the life of a doctor's wife.

The hours during residency are brutal. During intern year, I saw my husband on a nightly basis when his eyes were closed! He was working 80-plus hours a week, including weekends.

How did she cope?
1. She found a job that kept her busy during days and some weekends.
2. She made friends with wives of residents.
3. She made friends with young women not associated with residency.

After having children:
1. She stayed at home for the best of the children.
2. She was available to her husband *when* he was able to come home.
3. She joined a church Bible study.
4. She attended Wednesday night family church supper with or without her husband.
5. She formed a play group.
6. She joined the Junior League.

I am able to continue my life and yet be home when my husband comes home.

She concludes:

It is tough being the wife of a resident, but it is not forever! I work so hard on making sure everything is taken care of before he gets home so that he can enjoy his down time. I don't always get everything done. The house is usually a mess! But I have learned to be patient. When he is so dog-tired, the questions and bills can wait for another day. I believe I have the best relationship with my husband. Though I do not see him all the time, I know he loves me and I love him. He works very hard and it will all be worth the training one day. I just have to remember that this is God's plan and we just follow His footsteps!

—married five years

Establishing Couple Friends

No one ever told me about this when I got married. When you get married, you become a team and, luckily, you have a built-in date for Friday night as well as important black-tie functions! Being married is lovely (blah, blah, blah).

But what about your friends, and how do they fit into your life? Maybe your readers are more easygoing than I am, and you plan on taking all of your husband's friends into your circle of bosom buddies, but that is not how it was for me. Although I love these girls and like spending time with them, I have found that all of them are not the way I see my lifelong postcollege friendships going, and they merely serve to pass the time enjoyably rather than being trusted female confidantes and people who make you truly laugh. (You should understand this distinction.)

Now, you may think, what's the big deal? I can just spend time with my friends from college/high school and also include my husband's friends in a nice moderate social mix where we can split the time. Sadly, it is not so. Weekends are precious and free time is valuable. Additionally, as many women find, *we* are much more likely to incorporate our husband's friends into our lives than our husbands are to incorporate our friends. This is a real problem that usually ends in the fight with me saying to my husband, "How come you never like to hang out with *my* friends but we are always with *yours?*" Then, because I do have a wonderful husband, an effort is made for about two weeks and then we fall back into the usual pattern.

Now, here comes the glimmer of hope. I feel that I have the right as a newlywed to dispense this tidbit because I have seen the light. We found a tried-and-true, pure-and-fair couple, and they are our friends (we met our "couple friends" while doing laundry in our apartment building). To do this, *and it is important,* you as a couple should make a serious effort to step out of your proverbial boxes and start looking for these couple friends. Church groups and Bible studies are often good ways to meet couples that are new to both of you and have like-minded interests. I also recommend throwing a dinner party with the intention of meeting some of your friends' friends. Happy hunting!

—married one year

Control Release

Well, marriage is exciting and fun and especially so when you first begin your journey. I learned a great truth in the very beginning. I was happy and experiencing the best time of my life as a newlywed. However, I had this deep desire to leave my home and head off to the missions field. My husband and spiritual leader of the family was not feeling the same. I took it upon myself to change his mind, and it became a point of tension. I began to get frustrated. Other couples I knew were fussing over the typical stuff: how the toilet paper hangs, which end of the toothpaste to squeeze, and where the laundry should land. Instead, the only time we would ever disagree was when we would talk about missions. Well, finally one day I heard the Lord telling me to let go. I called my husband, crying from the bathroom of the little school where I taught, and apologized for trying to manipulate him. I don't think he even knew what I was talking about, but I knew what was in my heart. I let the Lord work and my husband lead. And the Lord moved fast! He may not always work this fast, but I think He wanted to encourage me this time.

Not long after, I was sitting across the table listening to my husband tell me the Lord was calling us as a couple to serve overseas, and I was wondering who I was talking to! It was more amazing than I could ever imagine. We were on the other side of the world in a matter of months, both using our talents in a way we enjoyed. He impressed me every day, the way he handled situations, relating to people, the work accomplished. I had no idea how incredible he is. God is in control. Release everything to the Lord, the things you want the most, even when you believe they are right. Allow Him to move in your marriage. He prepares and changes hearts.

—married four years

Remarriage

The best way to sum up divorce and remarriage, especially when children are involved, is "complicated." Even under the most favorable situations, it is complicated.

How to survive and thrive:
1. Lean on Jesus.
2. Unreal expectations have to go.
3. Junk your own agenda.
4. Don't take things personally.
5. Don't expect the Brady Bunch.
6. Be aware that extra baggage causes more dynamics.

—married five years

Marriage is a lot like decorating a house. More advice from the decorator:

Avoid being too "matchy." Be creative and mix old and new together. No suites of anything. That's the easy way out. Blending is the key to everything! One of my biggest pet peeves is to hurry and decorate a room with stuff to get by for a year or two . . . no no no. I would rather walk in and see an empty room with a fabulous chair or table and know that you are slowly building your room correctly than see a room full of stuff.

Marriage is a combination of two lives. The old is becoming new as two very different and imperfect people are now one. It takes a while to make this empty house become a beautiful, harmonious home, and the getting there includes better and worse.

Whatever the stage, the fire must be kept burning.

seventeen

Keep the Fires Burning

"He who finds a wife finds what is good and receives favor from the LORD."

—Proverbs 18:22

No matter how deeply a young married couple loves each other at the time of their marriage, there will be times when they simply will not like each other. This is important to know at the onset so that safeguards can be put into place, which help to protect the marriage.

My husband and I have had our share of ups and downs, like most married couples. Our most difficult problem is not to be roommates or two ships passing in the night. We are both so busy working, managing, balancing children, exercise, social obligations, etc., that our biggest fault is not giving each other any time. This is horrible to admit, but we can go for days without real conversation that doesn't pertain to kids, finances, or daily tasks. No excuses, but there is so much to do in one day that it never gets done. It's a vicious cycle that starts over every day. He leaves for work. I scramble to get the kids where they have to be with all their paraphernalia, start my workday, attend all dance shows, swim meets, school events, doctors' appointments, etc., then pick up dinner for the family, shove it down, start the cleaning and bathing process, get books read, prayers said, emails returned, then fall backwards into bed exhausted!

—married ten years

How important to feed your marriage. Focus on simple, planned, and purposeful actions that can help your marriage to grow. Strengthen and rekindle your love by spending time together. This is especially important if you have children.

Life became very busy for me when I got married at the age of 23. I started graduate school nine months after getting married. Then my husband and I had our first child the day before our two-year anniversary. We had our second child when we had been married for four and a half years. By the time we had been married five years, we had fixed up two houses and moved into our third. All that said, it is easy for life to get very busy as you become focused on the goals that you and your husband have for yourselves and your family. As a result, the best advice I could give about marriage would be to make the effort and to take the time to have date nights with your husband, especially when life is really busy. It is easy to become focused on your children and everything that you have going on, but it is so important to take time for each other.

—married eight years

Make your marriage the priority over your children. My parenting will never be as good as my marriage, but if I make my husband my priority, my children will greatly benefit. The greatest thing I can do for my children is to admire and respect my husband. The first thing I should put on my to-do list every day is to serve my husband. Ask him what I can do for him each day and try my best to deliver!

—married five years

Remember that love is an action. It is not always a feeling. You will not feel that heart-stopping, knock-you-off-your-feet kind of love all the time. You will go through dry spells. This is normal. After having children, your marriage will be stretched even more. Having children is wonderful, but it will test your marriage as views differ on issues involving the children. The key is communication, and that means making time for each other. Keep dating.

When my husband and I were dating, we would do fun little things for each other. For example, he might leave a note on my car or I might bring him cookies at work. It is all part of the dating game and trying to "catch" each other. I think it is important to keep doing those things once you are married—to keep the relationship fun and exciting. We will leave little notes hidden around the house when one of us goes out of town, so that the other one will find them while one of us is gone. My husband will bring me flowers for no reason, or I'll bake him a dessert for fun. These little acts of love can keep the romance alive.

—married three years

Ideas for Date Nights

1. Go for a long walk in a park and ask each other questions about dreams and ambitions.
2. Take a day trip to another town and spend the day exploring.
3. A cheeseburger and a movie can be the best night ever—if you leave bills and house problems at home.
4. Sometimes skip the wedding reception and treat yourself to a nice dinner out.
5. Some people might find it difficult to have a formal date night. What about a lunch date? What a great break in the middle of your day.
6. Be spontaneous, like when you were dating.
7. Drive-in movies are making a comeback.
8. Look in the newspaper for local events to go to.
9. Plan a date around what your husband likes to do.

10. Order dinner in.

11. Watch a video and snuggle on the sofa.

Dates are wonderful, but sometimes love can be expressed in other tangible ways.

> My husband expresses himself much more in writing than in conversation. One of my favorite things he does for me is to leave notes on my mirror, through email, and sometimes even in the mail.
>
> —married three years

Intimacy is so important, and that means keeping the TV out of the bedroom—your romantic haven. And one woman shares the benefit of owning only one TV.

> Don't own more than one TV. This may seem silly or impractical to many people who have the resources to buy more than one set, but this small, simple choice can teach you bigger and more important lessons in your marriage. It is very easy to be selfish about things like your preferred TV-watching sched-ule. Instead of owning two or more TVs so that each of you can watch what you want, isolated from one another, try compromising over these little matters like what show you will spend time watching. Learn to share; learn to give up this small desire of your own for the sake of your spouse. These minor lessons in compromise and sacrifice will lay the groundwork for when you and your husband face larger life issues that will require sacrificial love.

But beyond learning to share your time and your things, you will also get to know one another better, and it is such an easy way to spend time together that most of us already do! My husband and I have learned even more about one another by watching each other's shows. When I think of people I have known who have been married for many years, and who spend their evenings sitting by themselves in their separate rooms watching their separate TVs, it is such a sad picture.

Another benefit of learning to share the TV with your husband is that once kids come along, you as parents will have already set the standard for use of resources like the TV, and you can teach your children to be unselfish with their material things. As you teach them to share and to give and to spend time together, you will be adding to your foundation for healthy and loving family interaction.

—married four years

Have three nights during the week when the TV is not turned on at all. It can take the talk out of a relationship.

—married three years

1. Invest in fun books about dating and sex after marriage. Read them aloud together.
2. Journal about your day and exchange journals with your spouse.
3. Always celebrate your anniversary. You don't have to spend a lot of money or give expensive gifts to celebrate the special day. My husband

and I go to dinner on our anniversary every year. We have a special book that we were given during our engagement that we write in every year on our anniversary. We write down memories from the past year of our marriage. It can be anything such as moving, getting new pets, little trips we went on, weddings of friends, etc. It is so much fun to read back as the years go by, and it is amazing the little things that you can forget that happened in the past.

4. Call during the day just to let your spouse know you are thinking about him or to say, "I love you."

—married two years

The idea is to nourish and feed the marriage by intentionally and lovingly responding to the needs of each other.

A young woman shares her struggles of being married to a man who is in law school. She recognizes her shortcomings and strives to be the best wife and encourager she can be.

I'm the type of person who always tries to be kind, thoughtful, and considerate to other people, especially the ones I don't know well. Recently it really hit me how I was treating my husband in comparison to others. I'm embarrassed to say that I was not showing him the basic kindness that you would show a complete stranger. If I was stressed out, I would take it out on him—in the way I spoke, my mannerisms, and my reactions to him. It's so easy to completely let down around the people you love most. What I realized is that this is the love of my life, my best friend, and partner—didn't he deserve better than others? Well, he *does*, and this is something I've been changing for the past few months. It's amazing the difference it has made in our marriage. I don't always feel like doing this, but I made the choice to do these different things:

1. Actively listen when my husband is sharing something with me.
2. Speak to him kindly and lovingly instead of quickly and sharply.
3. Do little things that will help his day go better.
4. Not always complain to him about my day.
5. Encourage him vocally as well as praise his accomplishments.
6. Ask him to do something, rather than tell him.

—married three years

We (as Christian women) know that we are to study and grow in the knowledge of God's Word. If we are not relying on God, it will negatively impact those in our household! But we must also remember that we should grow in our knowledge of our husbands! We should study the man we married, learn more and more about him as each year passes in our marriage. If we do this correctly, we should be a more effective encourager, lover, servant, and friend to our husbands.

—married five years

Marriage is a wonderful gift. It is fun to be able to share your life with your best friend. There will be difficult times. With God's help, you will be able to get through them. Marriage at its best is a three-person relationship: husband, wife, and God. Pray *with* each other. Pray *for* each other. Share together. Grow together. Always keep in mind that you are in this together and on the same team.

> I certainly believe that my husband is more perfect for me and more wonderful than I could have imagined, but it is in more mature, less romantic, and less idealistic ways that I think so. We live day by day, and we commit each day to loving each other as God intends for us to do. It is because our relationship is *more* real and *more* true in those respects that it is tender, wonderful, and more than I could have asked for. Because the Lord's hand was in the construction of our relationship (because He allowed it to begin, continue, and thrive), we took utmost confidence in deciding that He, too, is well pleased with our decision to marry, and our daily commitment to each other and to our marriage.
>
> —married two years

"Therefore what God has joined together, let man not separate."

—Matthew 19:6

Contributors to
To Knot or Not

Virginia Hanson Apple (Ben)
Ashley Kensinger Batcheller (Christian)
Courtney Lukens Baxley (Charlie)
Tamzen Wagner Benfield (Trey)
Catherine McIntosh Bentley (Paul)
Georgi Deerman Bragg (Greg)
Wellon Lee Bridgers (Stephen)
Heather Carleton Brock (Stratton)
Kelley Brown Brown (Scott)
Rachael Broom Barnhart (John)
Katie McLure Bruce (Robert)
Mary Glen McPherson Carlton (Patrick)
Fran Coshatt Chaiprakob (Jeff)

Jill Suitts Coleman (Bryan)

Lori Pennington Cooper (Dave)

Jeanne Upchurch de'Laureal (Martin)

Cori Busbee Dillon (Daniel)

Kathleen Gibson Dragan (Grant)

Kathryn Miliron Dumas (Paul)

Susan Speir Dumas (George)

Amy Slappey Duncan (Ryan)

Kirsten Gladding Dunlap (John—"Boots")

Mallie Kidd Earl (Mark)

Libby Wood Greene (Chris)

Emily deFuniak Gregory (Paul)

Pat Clark Hammond (Terry)

Anca Curic Hanson (Robert)

Kristin Ziel Haushalter (Brandon Lee)

Julia Simmons Healey (Kyle Glenn)

Kari Schliesser Holley (Jason)

Shannon Upchurch Holt (Ted)

Lisa Bunting Howard (Harrison)

Annie Thompson Ingram (John)

Rachael McIntosh Jordan (Todd)

Robyn Caldwell Kown (Charles)

Jinnie Webster Lacey (Chris)

Alison Wilbourne Lagarde (Ross)

Katie Baker Lasker (Jim)

Catherine Caldwell Lipsey (Jayson)

Mallie Ireland Lynn (George)

Kit Upchurch McCaffery (Ryan)

Debbie Hunter McGillicuddy (Francois)

Kate Adams McKnight (Tom)

Beth Renneker McMillan (Murphy)

Caroline Dumas Malatesta (J. T.)

Lucy Thompson Marsh (Jacob)
Kimberly Guy Mason (Stephen)
Ginger Logue Menendez (Josh)
Tara Springfield Miller (Beau)
Dana Miserez Mixer (Chris)
Maggie Carter O'Conner (Tyler)
Courtney Johnson Pardue (Jarod)
Katie Sandlin Petrella (John)
Bradford Greene Phelan (Stephen)
Mona Gribbin Ponder (Trent)
Elizabeth Sandner Rich (Rusty)
Brooke McGuyer Sevier (Chris)
Corinna Saunders Slaughter (Kevin)
Graham Frankel Smith (Harrison)
Meeghan Callahan Sowinski (Grant)
Laura Glenn Steele (Parker)
Katie McKewen Smith (Doug)
Kristi Thomas Stein (John)
Lauren Holderfield Tanner (Brian)
Neillie Kirk Tayloe (Graham)
Michelle Bargeron Taylor (Scott)
Katherine Mellen Trammell (Buddy)
Ashley McLeod Turner (John)
Sarah Beth Davis Vines (Brian)
Rushton Mellen Waltchack (Derek)
Clayton Kearse Walton (Brandon)
Brooks Chappelle Wellmon (Chad)
Rhonda Pearce White (Chris)
Ashley Brock Wood (Claude IV—"Tapper")
Corinne Vann Wood (Leslie)

Other books by Donna Margaret Greene

Growing Godly Women: A Christian Woman's Guide to Mentoring Teenage Girls

twentysomething girl: real advice on relationships, careers, and life on your own

New Hope® Publishers is a division of WMU®, an international organization that challenges Christian believers to understand and be radically involved in God's mission. For more information about WMU, go to www.wmu.com. More information about New Hope books may be found at www.newhopepublishers.com. New Hope books may be purchased at your local bookstore.

BOOKS TO RESTORE YOUR
SOUL

Refresh
Sharing Stories. Building Faith.
Kathy Escobar and Laura Greiner
ISBN-10: 1-59669-069-0
ISBN-13: 978-1-59669-069-1

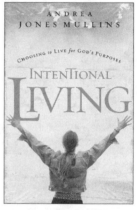

Intentional Living
Choosing to Live for God's Purposes
Andrea Jones Mullins
ISBN-10: 1-56309-927-6
ISBN-13: 978-1-56309-927-4

Engaged!
A Devotional to Help a Bride-to-Be Navigate Down the Aisle
Sandy Lovern
ISBN-10: 1-59669-035-6
ISBN-13: 978-1-59669-035-6

Available in
bookstores everywhere

For information about these books
or any New Hope product, visit
www.newhopepublishers.com.